THE ILLUSTRATED GUIDE TO WITCHCRAFT

THE ILLUSTRATED GUIDE TO
WITCHCRAFT

SACRED SITES, RITUALS, CELEBRATIONS
AND ILLUSTRATIONS

BY GRAHAM WYLEY

PARKGATE
BOOKS

First Published in Great Britain in 1998
by Parkgate Books Ltd, Kiln House,
210 New Kings Road, London SW6 4NZ

Copyright © Parkgate Books Ltd 1998

Text copyright © Graham Wyley 1998

British Library Cataloguing in Publication Data:
A CIP catalogue record for this book is available from the British Library.

ISBN 1 902616 00 6

Designed by Paul Vater at Sugar Free
Printed and bound in China

ACKNOWLEDGMENTS

In my work for this book I received a great deal of help and support from Witches and pagans who, not only invited me into their homes, granted interviews and furnished me with illustrations, photographs and material but included me in their seasonal celebrations and allowed me to participate in their secret coven rituals. To those witches who wish to remain anonymous I offer my sincere thanks for your kindness. I am also grateful for the cooperation and generosity of the following persons and establishments: Graham King and Liz Crow, Peter E. Pracownik, Cassandra Latham, Mistley Library, Animal Sanctuary, Mistley, Adrian Bryn-Evans, Ann Bryn-Evans (illustrator), Lauren Bladon-Gardner, Reg and Dot Griffiths, Peter Jennings, Diane Firmin, Ipswich Museum, Museum of Witchcraft, Boscaslte, Robin Herne, Doreen Valiente, Jenny Tucker, Emma Restallor (Bobcat), Philip Smallcross (Wolf Walks with Fire), Tyna Redpath, Mike Howard, Fay Cullen, Rose Thomas and Keith Morbey.

If I have omitted anybody, please accept my apologies, it is in no way intentional.

THE ILLUSTRATED GUIDE TO
WITCHCRAFT

CONTENTS

INTRODUCTION

If the average person were asked to describe a witch, they would probably tell you that witches do not exist. Witches, they will say, are imaginery, unkempt old women with black conical hats, warts on their noses, bad teeth and broomsticks, who are believed to create evil spells. The description has become curiously detailed, for a character who does not exist. This stereotype image would be more in keeping with the wicked witch in The Wizard Of Oz, nevertheless, this is the type of characterization that most people would use.

Any thought that there could be a male counterpart rarely enters into the equation. When it does, the word Warlock springs to mind. The term Warlock derives from the Old English *waer* 'truth' and *leogan* 'to lie'. Originally it meant any oath-breaker or traitor. In 1460 the term was equated with 'witch', culminating in the word being applied to both sexes. Although greatly outnumbered by their female counterparts, male witches have existed for centuries. In modern terminology the correct definition is cunning man.

Popular ideas about witchcraft, based on the gross exaggerations of centuries past, have been largely shaped by the media. The little that is known about witchcraft usually resolves itself into the statement that if witches do exist, they must be evil. Even today there is a large percentage of the general public who still retain the archaic presumption that all witches are evil-doers who delight in putting on spells and curses, worship Satan and recite the Lord's Prayer backwards.

The phrase "I don't believe in witches...but they exist!" highlights the contradiction that surrounds the belief in witches. Conflict and false reasoning occur due to the superstition which has always affected knowledge and opinions of witchcraft. This is sustained by its indefinable nature, that can be ascribed, in part, to the use of 'unseen' forces.

Magic is the art of effecting change through an external and supernormal force. The earliest evidence of magic dates from cave paintings of the Paleolithic Age, which indicate that magical rituals were employed to secure successful hunts.

Witchcraft, often called Wicca or the Craft, is considered to be one of the oldest religions. Emanating out of paganism, its nature-based beliefs revert back to a time when man was dependent on what the earth provided for survival.

Even those who are not so adamant in their opinions about witchcraft's existence still find that the word 'witch' conjures up the fear associated with mystery, magic, spell-casting and an involvement with the occult.

The fact that witchcraft has been, and still is, a secretive form of worship and devotion has contributed towards the intrigue surrounding the Craft. There is a tendency to prejudge the unknown and mysterious, because of the inexplicable circumstances involved, and this is particularly true of witchcraft.

What constitutes a witch? The supernatural is often offered as a consideration, once the 'old hag' concept is dismissed. Witchcraft is occasionally thought to involve supernatural powers, even though the boundary between the natural and the supernatural is continually being adjusted by scientific investigation.

It is possible to understand the involvement of hereditary witches following in their parent's tradition, but why should an individual seek initiation into the secret roll of a solo or coven participating witch?

The wise-woman of old had an important part to play in the community. She was the herbalist who made medicines, the midwife and the layer-out of the dead. She was also the old crone who kept herself to herself. This, by its very nature, made her a person of mystery.

The cauldron, black cat and broomstick became her trademarks. The belief that she could fly or turn a toad into a Prince has never really diminished, so with such a past reputation, why has the witchcraft tradition not only survived, but gained popularity in the ensuing years?

Devotees to the Craft strongly believe that the planet Earth must be respected at all costs, especially now, when its environment is being destroyed by mankind. This is the basis of their worship. These ecological concerns do not invalidate the fact that they are still capable of raising a cone of energy within a coven circle and using its magic for spell or charm-casting in a positive direction.

Let me state catergorically, to those of you who are still dubious about the existence of witches, that they have existed since the beginning of time and are as active today as they have ever been. They are still treated with contempt and caution and subjected to the stigma they have had to tolerate for centuries.

With the advent of Christianity, The Horned God that they worshipped was deemed to be the Devil. This accusation was so well deployed that witchcraft has never been able to live down its implications. For almost three centuries the fear of the witch's capabilities and the belief that these were coupled with satanic practices resulted in the persecution and annihilation of millions of witches throughout the world. Even this failed to stamp out something that was considered to be a threat to Christianity. The witchcraft movement continued, becoming more secretive to avoid reprisals, which possibly explains why modern witches do not advertise for applicants to join the craft.

In order for me to understand the purpose, beliefs, traditions and myths surrounding witchcraft more fully, it became necessary for me to gain the confidence of witches throughout the United Kingdom and participate in their ritual covens and celebrations.

Eventually, after entering into this veil of secrecy, I was able to discover that not only does magic exist, in the form of spells and charms, but that the use of the power of the mind for healing and the alteration of life's circumstances is a reality.

There is no doubt that the international religion of witchcraft is exceptionally well supported. The attraction of coven involvement is on the increase and even the initiation of solo witches continues in today's society.

Participants explain that by entering into the world of witchcraft they have achieved a greater understanding of life, a discovery of their inner self and a religion that is personal and not dogmatic. Through a sincere devotion to the Craft they have become able to control unseen forces for the good of mankind. . . Could this explain why people are attracted to the Craft?.. and what constitutes a witch?

BIBLIOGRAPHY

BARBER, Chris, *Mysterious Wales* (Granada Publishing, 1983)

BOURNE, Lois, *Witch Amongst Us* (St. Martin's Press, New York, 1985)

BUCKLAND, Raymond, *Buckland's Complete Book of Witchcraft* (Llewellyn Publications, St Paul, 1986)

------------, *Witchcraft Ancient and Modern* (Castle Books, Secaucus, NJ)

CROWLEY, Aleister, *Magick in Theory and Practice* (Privately published by Lecram Press, Paris, 1929. First authorised reprinting under title Magick by Routledge & Kegan Paul, Ltd, 1973, edited by John Symonds and Kenneth Grant)

GARDNER, Gerald B., *A Goddess Arrives* (Arthur Stockwell, 1939)

------------, *High Magic's Aid* (Michael Houghton, 1949)

------------, *Witchcraft Today* (Rider, 1954)

------------, *The Meaning of Witchcraft* (Aquarian Press, 1959)

GUILEY, Rosemary Ellen, *The Encyclopedia of Witches and Witchcraft* (Facts on File, New York and Oxford, 1989)

HOWARD, Michael A., *The Cauldron* (Mike Howard Publications, 1997)

JONES, Kelvin I., *Witchcraft in Cornwall* (Oakmagic Publications, 1995)

JONG, Erica, *Witches* (Harry N. Abrams, 1981)

LEEK, Sybil, *Diary of a Witch* (Leslie Frewin, 1975)

------------, *The Complete Art of Witchcraft* (London* New York, 1971)

MICKAHARIC, Draja, *A Century of Spells* (Samuel Weiser, York Beach, Me, 1988)

MONTER, E. William, *European Witchcraft* (John Wiley & Sons, Inc, 1969)

------------, *Witchcraft in France and Switzerland* (Cornell University Press, 1921)

PAGAN FEDERATION, The, *Witchcraft Information Pack,* (Pagan Federation, London, 1996)

RUSSELL, Jeffrey B., *A History of Witchcraft* (Thames & Hudson, 1987)

SANDERS, Maxine, *The Witch Queen* (Star Books, 1976)

SERGEANT, Philip W., *Witches & Warlocks* (Senate, 1996)

SKELTON, Robin, *The Practice of Witchcraft Today* (Robert Hale, 1988)

VALIENTE, Doreen, *An ABC of Witchcraft Past and Present* (Phoenix Publishing, Custer, Wash, 1986)

------------, *The Rebirth of Witchcraft* (Phoenix Publishing Inc, 1989)

WESIMAN, Richard, *Witchcraft, Magic and Religion in Seventeenth Century Massachusetts* (The University of Massachusetts Press, 1984)

CHAPTER ONE
IS WITCHCRAFT A RELIGION?

Below: The consort of the mother Goddess, the Horned God.

The very word witchcraft, or Wicca as it is also known, has been responsible for striking apprehension and terror into the hearts of innocent people for centuries. These people are convinced that magic, spell-casting and the pre-cognitive abilities represent the dark side of occult practice.

This is similar to the old superstition that if you are approached by a true Romany gipsy selling her wares you must not upset her, for you will invoke the curse of bad luck. Witchcraft, with its unknown capabilities, provokes an even more sinister prejudice in the minds of the general public.

There is no doubt that spirituality and magic have always formed the basis of witchcraft and the presumption that witches have mysterious powers has caused them to be persecuted throughout the ages. A witch is a person who follows the 'Old Religion' which he or she believes to pre-date Christianity. Religion is a belief in a superhuman being, a personal God. It is also the observance of practices derived from a system of faith, doctrine and worship, spiritual awakening and devotion. Witchcraft is no exception to this but unlike most religions, converts are never sought and initiation is never offered. Initiation is only given to those who have proved themselves. It is traditional to wait a year and a day before being accepted into the craft.

Witchcraft is both the oldest of all religions and one of the youngest. To this day it is still a developing religion. Long before the building of Stonehenge, the Goddess and her consort were being worshipped as they are in modern times.

Since prehistoric times people have worshipped celestial beings very different from those that are revered today. Many religions, with their countless Gods and Goddesses have come and gone, but the age-old Mother Goddess of the Earth and Triple Moon and her consort, the Horned God, has survived them all.

The Concise English Dictionary tells us that the word witchcraft is derived from the Old English *wiccacraft* or *wiccecraft*, the Way of the Wise or Wisecraft. This underlines the fact that its skill and procedure must be learned through dedication.

> Witchcraft is both the oldest of all religions and one of the youngest. To this very day it is still a developing religion.

Force of Nature by Peter E. Pracownik.

Right:
Feathered ritual mask,
symbolic of flight.

Witches have
always followed a
nature-based
spirituality and
honoured the 'Old
Gods'. Since the
Gods dwell within
nature, the
preservation of the
earth is crucial
and a strong
ecological
awareness is
maintained by
them.

Witches have always followed a nature-based spirituality and honoured the 'Old Gods'. Since the Gods dwell within nature, the preservation of the earth is crucial and a strong ecological awareness is maintained by them.

Wicca (witchcraft) is one of the major Pagan traditions which is not dogmatic but pursues its own vision of the Divine as a personal and direct experience. It is sometimes referred to as neo-paganism. Wiccans (witches)

Above: This ancient cauldron blew up on that fateful night when three determined participants succeeded in calling up ABADDON, the demon of hellfire!

worship what is often thought of as the Universal Life-Force or God in the form of the Goddess and the God. This God has often been portrayed as having horns, cloven hooves and a forked tail and defined as being the Devil, or Satan. However, the Horned God of the Wiccans is nothing to do with Satan. Wicca pre-dated Christianity, and the Horned God was ignored by the Church until the sixth century when he was identified as Satan and became a hate-figure in Christian perception. It was politically wise to classify the horned consort of the Goddess with the despicable representation of the Devil in order to discredit Wiccan worship.

Another explanation for this ongoing misconception derives from the times of persecution when witches were known to confess to having had intercourse with the Devil. In fact their relationship had simply been with the High Priest of the coven who wore a horned head-dress and cloak of skins at ritual ceremonies.

There are a varied range of traditions which have emerged from paganism. These include Witchcraft, Druidry, Odinists, Shamans and Goddess-worship.

Wicca (witchcraft) is one of the major Pagan traditions which is not dogmatic but pursues its own vision of the Divine as a personal and direct experience.

Above: A 'skyclad'
ceremonial ritual

These are nature-
based beliefs
which
acknowledge the
cycles of life, death
and rebirth with
particular
emphasis on the
phases of the sun
and moon.

All of these are nature-based beliefs with the common factor that they all have respect for the earth and its life-forms, they acknowledge the cycles of life, death and rebirth with particular emphasis on the phases of the sun and moon.

The humble peasant persisted in the practice of his chosen pagan beliefs long after Christianity became an established religion. Initially, Pagans out-numbered Christians, so the church had to tolerate paganism. Both deities were worshipped simultaneously, respecting each other's belief with a com-passionate reverence, to the extent that each had their own separate entrance and altar under the same church roof. The Pagan altar faced west or north, a practice still observed by many modern Pagans, and the Christian altar faced towards the east. This arrangement began to change as Christianity became the dominant religion. The next development was the systematic condemna-tion and persecution of Pagans.

These were fearful times. The Gods they had worshipped were denounced as 'Devils' by the Christians and their religious practices and beliefs were declared to be evil. The advent of determined eradication of their religion resulted in Pagans continuing to pay reverence to their old Gods in secret and was the beginning of reticent group meetings held on moors, in forests or in

Abduction of Prosperine (Persephone) on a unicorn. (Albrecht Durer 1516)

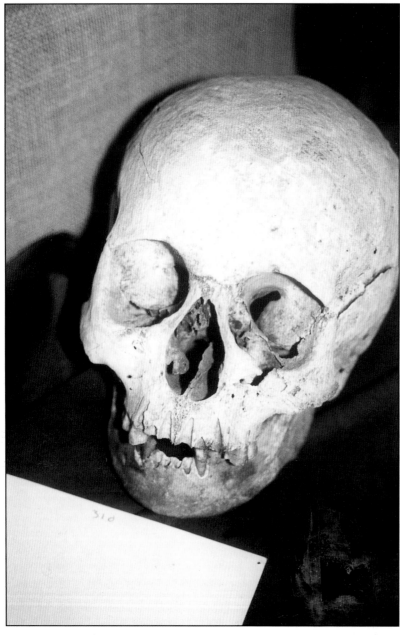

Above: A couple of years ago this skull was discovered in its stone inset shrine high up on the slopes of Bodmin Moor. A strange place. This moor is not so well known as Dartmoor and therefore less frequented by strangers for the most part. A place where prehistoric man is never far from you. A place where spirit contact is easier than most.

any concealed countryside. Paganism still thrived in what we today might describe as a secret society. Their acts of group worship were deemed to be covens and those who continued to practice the old religion were judged as witches.

The common myth of a union between the witch and the Devil has been immortalised in paintings and engravings over the centuries and still remains. Fear of the witch's magic and mystery has continued. During the Middle Ages it was believed that the witch had no hope of escaping the pact made with the Devil, for in return for his favours he would not fail to come and demand payment of her soul. These beliefs were also predominant in medieval iconography, which often depicted witches and sorcerers riding together on a goat or witches being carried away by devils. The Prince of Darkness was often represented as being mounted on a black horse which always gallops to the left, another sinister characteristic.

Ancient folklore and mythology offer a possible explanation to the idea of a connection between the Prince of Darkness and the puritanical maiden. They also suggest how this unusual pairing was associated with the seasons. The story goes that before time was measured, when the Gods walked the earth and conversed with Man, the Goddess Demeter, Lady of the Golden Grain and all of nature's bounty, bore a fair

The common myth of a union between the witch and the Devil has been immortalised in paintings and engravings over the centuries and still remains. Fear of the witch's magic and mystery has continued.

Left: A High Priest plunges the athame into the priestess' chalice of wine to symbolise the union between the male and female representatives of the God and Goddess.

daughter to the mighty Zeus. She named her child Persephone and loved her above all else. Persephone grew to be to be a gentle and beautiful young woman. All who saw her loved her, calling her Kore, the maiden, and the world was all the more wonderful for her presence. Such was her grace and charm that even the heart of Hades, the Dark Lord of the Underworld, was warmed and he burned with desire for her. One day as Persephone, innocent and carefree, gathered flowers in the meadows, the Dark Lord sprang up from the earth and spirited her away, down, down into the depths of his kingdom, far from the sunlight and all she knew and loved.

Witchcraft began to emerge publicly in its modern form in the late 1940s, hence the reference to it also being one of the youngest religions. Like so many other religions, its function was to point individuals or covens towards a greater understanding with the divine creative principle of the universe. There are four main traditions of the craft: Gardnerian Wicca, Alexandrian Wicca, Hereditary and Traditional Craft, each with its own practices and beliefs.

Demeter was desolate. She covered her beauty with a dark veil and travelled the wide world, searching tirelessly for her beloved daughter. As Demeter hid her face and mourned, the Earth suffered and became barren. The fields bore no grain and the vines no fruit.

Mankind, in fear and hunger, beseeched the Gods for aid. The Gods pleaded with Demeter to relent and bless the earth once more, but nothing would satisfy her but the return of her daughter.

Meanwhile Persephone roamed the corridors of Hade's palace, her beauty shining like the silver moon in the darkness, refusing all the gifts of the Dark Lord and eating nothing, for she feared that if she ate the food of Hades she would be compelled to remain with him forever. At last he was prevailed upon to release the maiden, but it seems that his great love for her must have found an echo in her heart, for he persuaded her to eat a few pomegranate seeds, which in ancient lore were a symbol of love and marriage. For it is true that although mankind fears the touch of Death, in the end his embrace brings release from the suffering, pain and sorrow of old age and disease and the spirit finds rest and healing in his Kingdom. Persephone felt his loneliness and need and her kind heart was moved.

When Demeter was reunited with her daughter she was filled with joy; but when she learned of the pomegranate seeds her heart was full of dread once more. The Gods debated long and hard; and a compromise was reached for the sake of the Earth. Persephone would spend one third of the year with her husband and two thirds with her mother.

And so it came about that every year the barren months of Winter are followed by the blessings of spring, when the whole world awakens to Demeter's joy at her daughter's return from the underworld.

THE ILLUSTRATED GUIDE TO WITCHCRAFT

Witchcraft began to emerge publicly in its modern form in the late 1940s, hence the reference to it also being one of the youngest religions. Like so many other religions, its function was to point individuals or covens towards a greater understanding with the divine creative principle of the universe. There are four main traditions of the craft: Gardnerian Wicca, Alexandrian Wicca, Hereditary and Traditional Craft, each with its own practices and beliefs. One common bond between them all was the acceptance that ritual sites, whether cast as circles or existing ancient locations, were sacred. Because

Below: The 5 pointed pentagram symbolises spiritual awareness together with the four elements of life.

their religion is nature-based, witches have always considered themselves as being among the first ecologists.

This harks back to the days when the first primates began their day when it became light and slept when darkness descended. There was a high rate of infant death due to illness. Babies would be placed in the cleft of a tree or behind a large rock safely away from wild animals. Those who survived had a life expectancy of a meagre thirty years.

In those times men understood that women brought forth life. Women were the procreators who tended the offspring and performed all the necessary duties from birth to death. They were, in fact, the wise-women. Man's role was that of hunter, farmer and provider.

Human progress worked with nature, with understanding of the changing seasons, when food was sparse or plentiful and the extreme changes of temperature when darkness or cold would descend. Man learned to use this knowledge of the seasons to his advantage. He began to

Originally pentagrams were used by ritual magicians who would inscribe them on wood, clay or metal and use them as a protection against the spirits that they had summoned. Witches, however, draw pentagrams in the air, with the sacred dagger (athame), at each of the four points of the circle in order to invoke the guardians of the elements of fire, water, earth and air. This nature-based approach is, and always has been, the keystone of the craft and it enables witches to conjure up the necessary ritual energies needed to perform their own ceremonial magic.

hunt, the prey supplying food and skins for body warmth and he began to plant seeds in harmony with Mother Earth. The rivers provided the water he needed, and the mystery of life-giving air may have been the starting-point for the concept of spirit.

Man had begun to realise that the natural elements at his disposal were necessary for his survival. The way in which these were used could well be interpreted as a form of magic. The four elements of earth, air, fire and water were the tools of his apprenticeship. They could promote longevity if used wisely.

As they sat round the fire together they began to realise that there was, magically speaking, strength in numbers. This configuration was all-important, for the circle sustained the energy of those present, which is why the ceremonial circle is sacred and still cast in rituals today.

In witchcraft the significance of the five-pointed pentagram is this: It is seen as one's own human awareness, spirituality being the uppermost point with the remaining points symbolising the four elements of life controlled by spirit. Originally pentagrams were used by ritual magicians who would inscribe them on wood, clay or metal and use them as a protection against the spirits that they had summoned. Witches, however, draw pentagrams in the air, with the sacred dagger (athame), at each of the four points of the circle in order to invoke the guardians of the elements of fire, water, earth and air. This nature-based approach is, and always has been, the keystone of the craft and it enables witches to conjure up the necessary ritual energies needed to perform their own ceremonial magic.

Wiccans believe that if anyone carries out a wicked act they should admit it and shoulder the blame themselves, not alleviate their guilt by shifting the responsibility onto some obnoxious, heathen and evil Prince of Darkness. Modern witches abide by the rule DO WHAT YOU WILL BUT HARM YE NONE. Should this be ignored, the result is likely to be threefold repercussions.

CHAPTER TWO
WITCHES WORSHIP & SABBATS

Witches revere the age-old Mother Goddess and her consort, the Horned God, who rule the universe together. These deities are mother and father figures who will bring happiness if appeased but will inevitably chastise if angered. The Goddess, in one or more of her aspects, has been present in many religions.

Above: Cernunnos, the Horned God.

Witches see her as representing three aspects of life, from birth to death; that of the young maiden, the mother figure and finally the bedraggled, one-toothed, ugly, story-telling wise old woman or crone, who is also the layer-out of the dead.

The creation of life is the result of the union of male and female. The God and Goddess represent the masculine and feminine principle on the divine level. Some Pagans pray, whereas Wiccans channel the strength and energy from their God and Goddess.

The Goddess is seen as ruling from spring until autumn and her consort during late autumn and winter. The names by which they are known vary from coven to coven but Cerridwen for the Goddess and Cernunnos, meaning

Horned One, or Herne for the God are the most popular. Often the deity names used by a coven are considered so sacred that they are only known as the Lady and Lord outside the consecrated ritual circle.

The worship of a mother-figure, the bearer of life, is as old as time itself. We know that she was the predominant deity in ancient Babylonia, over five thousand years ago, our ancestors worshipped her as the Queen of Heaven. Statues of the Goddess have been discovered dating as far back as 25,000 B.C. The adoration of the forces of nature, the belief that all living things have a soul and the idea of some sort of continuation of life after death such as reincarnation, are all ancient concepts.

Witchcraft practice is concerned with a re-linking with the life force of nature on this planet and even in the stars beyond. At full moons and Sabbats, Wiccan groups worship the Gods in order to revitalise their sense of coacting with the universe. They believe that when the various aspects of nature are celebrated, a re-awakening in ourselves and the world around us takes place.

In the eyes of her worshippers, the life cycle of the Goddess runs parallel to nature's changing seasons, beginning with her maidenly aspect in the Spring, followed by her wedding to the Horned God in Summer. At harvest-time she is the mother-figure, then in Autumn and Winter

Above: The Star card of the Tarot pack represents the Goddess in the aspect of Maiden, magically pregnant, as all life springs from her.

Right: Catweasel - Third Degree Wiccan Priest (defined by symbols on his Tabard) consulting his book of shadows.

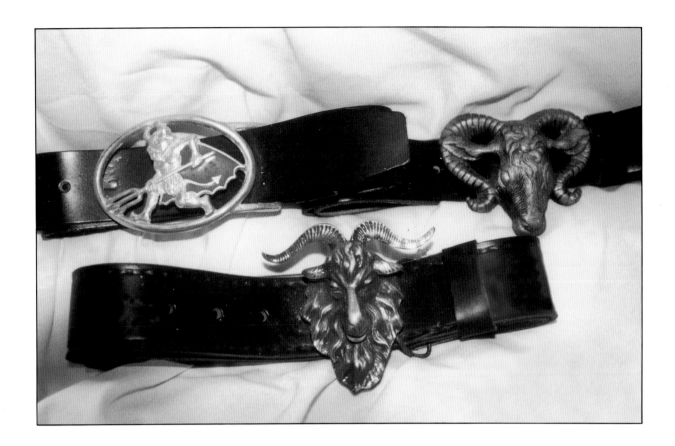

she becomes the crone, a wise-woman growing old with the inevitability of the receding year. As the next year arrives this process is repeated, for in the mystical religion of Wicca, the Goddess is eternal.

Above: Ceremonial belts depicting the Devil and the Horned God.

The masterful Horned God was a God of many idiosyncrasies. He enhanced reproduction in humans and animals, was responsible for plentiful crops and, when invoked, he bestowed magical capabilities upon his worshippers. He commanded that during these times there should be festivity, feasting, and excess in the joys of life. Yet his displeasure would result in the frightening repercussions of his voice booming through the skies like thunder. Pictorial descriptions of the Horned God can be found in Paleolithic cave paintings. This was a time when man imitated the appearance of the animal roaming in the forest, not entirely in order to simulate its gracefulness, but that this representation would open up a magical channel and enhance his hunting capabilities. In the Caverne des Trois Freres at Ariege in France, a painting of a prancing being dressed in the skin of an animal and wearing the horns of a stag can be clearly seen. It was not thought that there was anything evil about the Horned God, in fact primitive man ascribed everything good or evil for which he could find no logical explanation to him.

With the advent of Christianity, the Horned God's physical characteristics were transferred to the Devil, or Lucifer, and as a result of this association, he

Wiccan groups believe that when the various aspects of nature are celebrated, a re-awakening in ourselves and the world around us takes place.

To be aware when animals and birds were ready to breed, and most importantly, knowing the exact time to preserve food for the Winter to avoid starvation.

Approach without fear,
you who know me in your heart,
for I speak to you
with the voices of the winds
and the shoreline
is the hem of my robe.

I am the breath of hope
which is born in the East,
the Maiden,
the new morning,
the promise of Spring.

Mine is the power
which burns in the South,
the Mother,
the midday warmth,
the blessings of Summer.

I will draw you to me
as the day fades in the West,
the Wise Woman, the healer,
the mourner of the waning year.

And when the bitter wind
blows from the North,
bidding life withdraw,
to rest, to dream,
I beckon you as Crone,
as the Dark Mother,
the seed of life preserved
in the bare Earth,
from which you have been born
and will be born again.

acquired the Devil's evil ways. It is interesting to note that the word Lucifer is Latin for light-bearer, an entirely different interpretation to the one normally presented to us. It seems to have been confused with the Christian idea of the rebel archangel who fell from heaven whom we know as Satan. Nevertheless the seed had been sown and it grew into a permanent misconception. The God of the old religion became the Devil of the new. Evidence of this idea can be found as far back as A.D. 208, in the writings of a Roman historian and it has been fuelled by myths, chronicles, fear and persecution for over 1700 years. Even as we approach the 21st century, there is a generally held belief that witches work with the Devil.

The 'Wheel of the Year' defines the witches' Calendar, for although the waxing and waning of the moon are especially important times when energies are summoned for the casting of spells, the eight Sabbats are the predominant festivals.

These were celebrated long before Christianity. In those days survival depended on farming and hunting, so the changing seasons were an all-important factor in witches' lives. The concept of working within the seasons was the bible of the countryside. It was necessary to know when to sow and reap their crops, to be aware when animals and birds were ready to breed, and most importantly, knowing the exact time to preserve food for the Winter to avoid starvation. Because Pagans and witches existed by living with the land, they saw the earth as being the 'Great Mother' from whom they received the necessities for survival.

The Goddess who witches worship is primarily based on the Great Mother Earth of those ancient times and, in general terms, the Horned God is her husband and part-

Above: Green Man symbol.

ner. The Green Man is one of two other characters who feature in this yearly cycle. He is an aspect of the divine male principle and would have represented the spirit of nature at a time when people became more agricultural and although not a God himself, his importance was not to be underestimated. His representative duties in nature ran from Spring to Autumn, the period from sowing to harvesting. He has a wildness about him, but it is without violence.

Below: The congregation of two covens.

The Green Man's
breath is generally
depicted as
greenery bursting
out of his mouth.

Above:
Green man in
ceremonial
costume.

It is a wildness connected with the God Pan. The word 'panic', meaning an
overpowering fear, was derived from this God's name. An awareness of the
Green Man's power is often felt as an inexplicable perception in forests, or when
surveying the countryside's green vegetation. This feeling not only stimulates the
spirit, but makes one appreciate the irrepressible wonder of nature.

When displayed on masks or elsewhere, the Green Man's breath is generally
depicted as greenery bursting out of his mouth. At one time it was difficult to
find examples other than in books or churches. Here his likeness appeared
carved at the end of church pews or could be found at the feet of statues of the

Virgin Mary with Jesus. With modern day interest in ecological issues and concern about mankind destroying the planet, he is becoming more widely revered and symbolically important

The other character is the Lord of Misrule, who represents the lighter and more chaotic aspect of the Calendar. Many people become afraid of unexplained energy and are unable to cope with chaos, instead of understanding that it is part of life's natural sequence. The Lord of Misrule represents a surrounding energy which is spiritually active on the planet between Hallowe'en, the beginning of the traditional witches' Calendar, and Yule. His macabre rule begins on the festival which is celebrated all over the world as Hallowe'en, when the spiritual veil of life is at its thinnest, enabling greater communication with the spirits, which is also known as 'the festival of the dead'.

The symbolic term of office ascribed to the Lord of Misrule extends to Midwinter, or Yule, when, metaphorically, the spark of life begins to awaken. Between these times there is a limbo, an interval between death and rebirth, which is often considered to be a chaotic period.

Above: The Lord of Misrule displays the element of humour.

His origins may be in medieval times when a fool would have been elected by ballot to rule through the twelve days of Christmas. With his cap of jingling bells and armed with a weapon in the form of a pig's bladder, he could do just what he liked and no one could stop him. In some ways it was the serf's way of getting his own back on his master. The Lord of Misrule is the divine court jester, the magical representation of the element of humour.

Although witches profess that they honour all Gods throughout the religious spectrum, these four are the main characters on the stage of the witchcraft play of life.

The witches' Calendar is comprised of Sabbats which are the festivals celebrated by groups or covens eight times during the year. These are the times when rituals can include casting a circle at an ancient site, a reminder that the 'Old Ones' had, and still have, an immense knowledge of the lunar and solar cycles. A simple altar is fashioned as a focal point and the magical energies of the land are brought into the circle. Also, a closeness with the spirits of their ancestors is achieved and the coven's gratitude is shown by way of appreciative worship of their Gods and reverence of the four elements.

The Lord of Misrule represents a surrounding energy which is spiritually active on the planet between Hallowe'en, the beginning of the traditional witches' Calendar, and Yule.

Above: An entourage of Druids, Celts and Witches en route to their sacred site at a Sabbat.

Left: A congregation of Druids, Pagans, Celts and Witches.

Each Sabbat has it's own definite place in the earth's cycle. The wheel of the year is not just a matter of the changing seasons, beneath the outward structure there are subtle energy patterns which affect us all. By understanding the flow and direction of that energy, we can appreciate its harmony as true inhabitants of our planet.

At the commencement of the witches' Calendar is Hallowe'en, otherwise known as Samhain, and the Celtic equivalent of New Year's Eve. It is that time of the season when cold winter approaches, the trees become bare and the nights get darker. When Britain converted to Christianity many of the old festivals were renamed. Thus the All Saints (All Hallows) festival remembers the dead at the same time that witches celebrate Samhain. There is a sincere belief among the Wiccan fraternity that on this night the earth and the world of spirit are very close to each other, which enables contact to be made between them. Hence reference is often made to this time as being the night of the dead.

As the wheel turns through seasons of dearth and plenty, death and rebirth, each segment becomes a significant time for witches to express their wishes and give thanks for the passing season until the cycle becomes complete with the Autumn Equinox.

At this time of year the emphasis is on the harvest festival ritual of giving thanks to Mother Earth for the crops and produce that she has provided. Often a vast Congregation of Druids, Pagans, Celts and Witches will integrate for communal worship at a sacred site, share specially prepared bread and wine and offer their gratitude to the Gods of the four elements.

Witches also hold minor celebrations at the time of each waxing and waning moon, in the belief that a full moon increases the magical power of their spells, whereas the dark moon assists banishment in their magic.

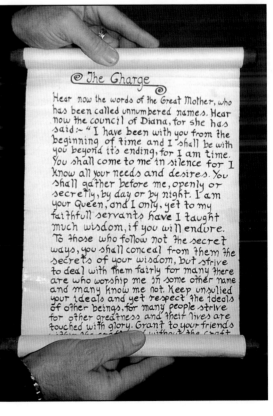

Top Right: Traditional baked sheaf-loaf distributed at tha Autumn Equinox.

Right: The charge is read out between the beginning of the ritual and the coven circle being cast.

THE WHEEL OF THE YEAR
THE WITCHES SEASONAL CALENDAR

OCTOBER 31ST:
Samhain or Hallowe'en

This is the night when spirits and people are at their closest. It is the official end of Summer and the beginning of Winter. It is a night of mischief.

DECEMBER 21ST:
Yule

This is the longest night of the year. It is a time for present-giving, festivities, rejoicing, decorating the house and putting up a tree to celebrate the enduring life force.

JANUARY 31ST
FeImbolc or Candlemas

As the sun becomes visible in the sky again, candles are lit to hasten its journey and also depict symbols of our own reawakening. It is a time for turning inward to clear the way for personal spiritual rebirth.

The Lord of Misrule presides over the yuletide celebrations.

Imbolc – Candlemas.

MARCH 21ST:
Spring Equinox

The length of day and night are now equal and spring begins to quicken the revived growth of plants and trees. New-born animals emerge to explore the world.

APRIL 30TH-MAY 1ST:
Beltane

The weather becomes warmer and the plants blossom. This is the time when people dance around the maypole. This is said to be a magical time of great power.

JUNE 21ST:
Midsummer

On this, the longest day of the year, light and life are plentiful. It is a time to look outwards, experience the joys of plenty and celebrate the fullness of the season.

At Beltane, the beginning of Summer, The Goddess prepares for her wedding to the Horned God.

JULY 31ST
Lughnasadh or Lammas

It is the feast of loaves at which the first grain harvest is consumed at a ritual meal and is also the time of the fire festival.

SEPTEMBER 21ST:
Autumn Equinox

This is the only other time of year when the day and night become equal. Harvest festivals are held to give thanks for the crops and produce which the earth has provided.

The Corn King Represents the sacrificed God at Lammas when, traditionally, harvest begins.

The two brothers, the Oak King and the Holly King, do battle at the Solstices for the love of the Goddess. The Oak King is victorious at the Summer Solstice and rules over the waning year, until he is defeated at the Winter Solstice by the Holly King, the Lord of the waxing year.

Herne the Hunter, Lord of the Wild Hunt rules over the winter months.

Requiem

That which belongs to Air
has returned to the East.
The Wheel turns
and Spring is over.

That which belongs to Fire
has returned to the South.
The wheel turns
and Summer has flown.

That which belongs to Water
has returned to the West.
The wheel turns
and Autumn passes.

That which belongs to Earth
has returned to the North.
The wheel turns
the Winter has ended.

That which belongs to Spirit
has returned to the old Ones.
The wheel turns
the Cauldron awaits.

That which belongs to fellowship and love-
that which belongs to Circle-
remains with us.
Nothing is final,
no farewell is the last.
The wheel turns,
and we, who tread the dance which never ends,
will share the gifts of food & wine again.

Ann C Bryn-Evans,
February '95

The above requiem was written to honour the passing of the
High Priest Hern on February 19th, 1995.

Top right: A witches' familiar called 'Midnight'

Above left: Statue of a traditional witch of a bygone era.

Above centre: A carving of a bygone witch, her name was Meg Marrilles.

CHAPTER THREE
WHAT IS A WITCH?

It is often imagined that witches are like the characters who appear in children's fairy stories. The normal image is of an elderly, wrinkled creature with long, untidy hair, a large pointed nose with a grotesque wart and grubby fingernails.

She wears a large, pointed and crumpled felt hat which matches the black of her dress. Her companion is a fierce-looking black cat that invariably travels with her on her broomstick. She is the bringer of retribution through the use of spell-casting magic which she concocts by toiling over a foul-smelling cauldron.

This description is not so far from the truth when we realise that the witch of old, who might be remembered by our great-grandparents, would be a wise-woman who lived alone in a cottage on the outskirts of a village. These were the women who looked after the midwifery and the laying-out, the birthing and the deaths. They were the problem solvers and healers . . .

In those days many villages were without doctors, so you would visit your village wise-woman for a potion or poultice made up of herbs and 'unmentionables' based on handed-down remedies. The witches and cunning men became the Citizen's Advice Bureau of the day, whether it be for ailments, illnesses, family problems or a dispute with your partner. Invariably, a trip to their lonely cottage proved to be the solution. The fear of their knowledge, and the power which they could command as a result of their importance, has contributed to the stereotype of a witch, a stereotype that has remained through the ages. They had a secret mystical power, which they called upon when administering their recommendations and potions. Their patients were simple country folk who received unconventional treatment which used, as part of its process, something that they considered to be magic. This caused them to look upon witches with a wary respect.

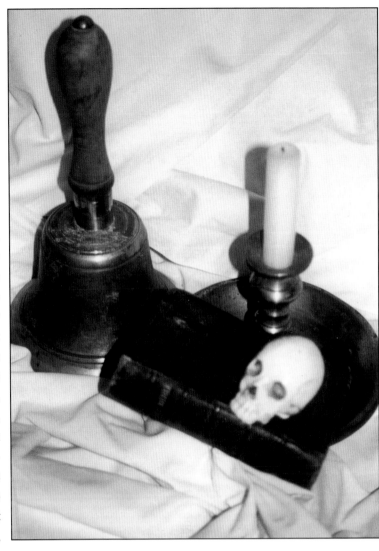

Above: Bell, Book and Candle. The conventional equipment used for warding off evil spirits.

Even today the dictionary definition of the word witch is 'A woman having dealings with evil spirits or practising the black art, or sorcery; a bewitching or fascinating woman, an old and ugly woman, a hag.' With this kind of generalisation it is hardly surprising that an awesome mental picture is created of this solitary and bizarre female figure, deliberating on her evil spells, her bedraggled appearance being singled out for persecution. Closer scrutiny of this definition reveals that the image of the old hag has been documented since ancient times. She is seen as primarily nocturnal and the hag phenomenon involves witches, demons, apparitions and inexplicable sounds. This is often accompanied by a feeling of paralysis and suffocation. Back in the Middle Ages this condition was attributed to witches or 'old hags' whom, it was believed, would sit on a person's chest during the hours of darkness and ride them. Their weight caused the person to experience exhaustion and suffocation - hence the term 'hag-ridden' or 'haggard' to describe the feeling of being run-down or gaunt from fatigue.

The magic of a witch is real. She can call up and focus mysterious powers and energies at will, for good or evil. It is gratifying to know that in most cases it is the former. In magical practice, the more formal kind of ritual is usually performed collectively, whereas the Hedge Witch works more intuitvely with herbs and magical ingredients. The Hedge Witch usually works alone - does not belong to a coven and is more shamanic and independent. Throughout history most witches, not necessarily by choice, have preferred this isolated existence in a dwelling away from prying eyes where they could conjure up their established remedies from their secret Book of Shadows (spells). In the past when many witches were unable to write, this information, handed down through the generations, was either committed to memory through continual use, or recorded using signs, colours and rough drawings. As literacy increased the Book Of Shadows became the encyclopedia of the coven, where ritual magic, details of an individual's accomplishments in that coven, poetry, prayers, spells and charms, would be hand-written. Eventually this would constitute a permanent record of the magical teachings.

A good example of this powerful magic was displayed in the 1920s by Hannah the witch who lived in the little village of Henley, near Membury in Wiltshire. Her cottage was located in the lower part of the village, close to a tiny stream, overlooked by a gnarled and curiously-shaped willow tree. Hannah regularly stood at her gate, demanding hand-outs, such as food, from people and insisting that any passer-by should collect sticks for her fire. She was, in fact, always worrying people and making a nuisance of herself. A farmer passed her cottage one day leading two horses. She confronted him, insisting that he fetch some wood for her fire. The farmer's reply was sharp and to the point as he continued on his way, "Not now. I've too much to do," he shouted, without even turning around. Arriving home he tethered the two horses to a gatepost and went inside. Upon his return, some fifteen minutes later he found both horses lying dead on the ground. Provoking the witch's displeasure was something to be avoided at all costs, as another neighbour, Miss Jane Harding, was to discover when passing Hannah's cottage late one night. In a challenging voice, the witch shouted out, "Have you got anything for me today?" Miss Harding replied courteously that she had nothing for her as she had been too busy to think of anything but her own duties that day. The very next morning when she arose, Jane Harding found that all of her turkeys, which she had lovingly reared for the dinner table, had died mysteriously!

The witches' ritual magic in its many forms was frighteningly reliable. Many

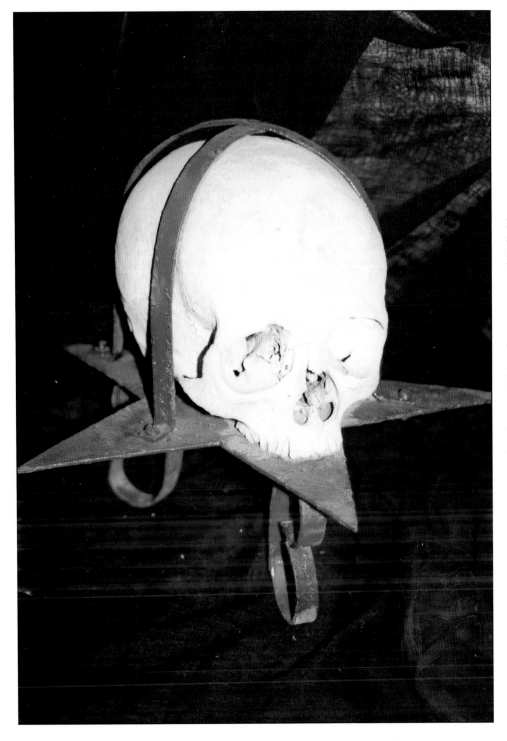

Left: The personal advisor of Old Granny Mann, the Witch.

The witches' ritual magic in its many forms was frighteningly reliable. Many witches used to consult bizarre pieces of paraphernalia such as the ancient skull mounted on a star-shaped stand used by the witch of North Bovey, Devon.

witches' used to consult bizarre pieces of paraphernalia such as the ancient skull mounted on a star-shaped stand used by the witch of North Bovey, Devon. She used to keep her 'friend', as she called this relic, in a secret place upon Easdon Tor. Old Granny Mann, as she was known, when presented with a problem or difficult situation by her clients, would always say "Well my dear,

I don't rightly know off hand what I will do till I have asked my friend, then I'll let thee know what is to be done."

Often unusual characteristics determined the status of a witch. Joan Wytte, born in 1775, was one such lady who seemed to have earned this recognition. Local legend tells of a small woman from Exeter, Devon who had the power to foretell the future with uncanny accuracy for any person. She was prone to aggressive outbursts of bad temper and violence. During these rages she showed extraordinary strength for a woman of her meagre stature, by lifting and beating people three or four times her size and weight. It was considered that such a show of phenomenal strength by one so small could only be explained as the work of the Devil. The local population went in fear of Joan Wytte, the witch.

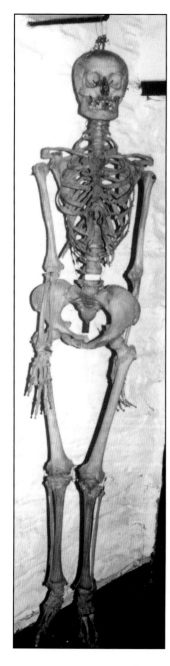

Below:
The skeleton of the Witch
Joan Wytte.

There have always been black and white witches. Those who prefer to work on the darker side of the occult use acts of magic contrary to the Craft's belief of 'DO WHAT YE WILL, BUT HARM YE NONE'. One of the first documented witches was the Witch of Endor who, according to the story related in Samuel 1 of the Old Testament, used Necromancy - the conjuring up of the dead, or the spirits of the dead, for magical purposes. This was at the request of King Saul of Israel who faced an impending attack by a mighty army of Philistines and, conviced that he had been abandoned by God, needed the spirit of Samuel to be raised fom the grave for prophecy and divination.

A Faerie Mother. The spirit world is often referred to as the "World of Faerie"

Unfortunately the media have always emphasised the sensational side of witchcraft, dwelling on the act of cursing and the idea that witches are sexually greedy. All witches have the ability to perform acts of either black or white. Most people consider that these abilities could be used to obtain power and wealth. They like the idea of possessing these magical powers and using them for their own selfish gain. They do not realise that the purveyor of magic is responsible for their own actions and that the misuse of power corrupts and destroys.

When a theatrical group in Plymouth were staging Shakespeare's

THE ILLUSTRATED GUIDE TO WITCHCRAFT

Unfortunately the media have always emphasised the sensational side of witchcraft, dwelling on the act of cursing and the idea that witches are sexually greedy.

Left: The Witch of Endor (right), summoning the ghost of Samuel for Saul.

Below: The fateful 'Macbeth' cauldron of Mother Whitchale.

'Macbeth', they borrowed an authentic cauldron with a mysterious history for the famous witches scene.

Later, members of the amateur group were affected by a whole series of tragic happenings. Soon a story was circulated that all the deaths and misfortunes of those associated with the

The White Witch
by Peter E.
Pracownik.

Wicca has always been a mystery religion. The details of rituals, or the names of any of the participants are never divulged to an outside party. This secrecy, witches will tell you, goes back to the days of persecution, the burning time.

group were due to using this cauldron of the witch, Mother Witchale.

This so upset the owner, that without telling anyone he took it out and dumped it, never telling anyone of its secret location to his dying day. In 1982 people with metal detectors were exploring Chelston Meadows, near Saltram House, the site of the long time closed and grassed over Plympton rubbish dump and they located the very same cauldron. It is now housed in the Witchcraft Museum in Boscastle, Cornwall.

William Shakespeare seems to have been well informed about witches' behaviour. He depicted the three witches in Macbeth gathering round their famous cauldron watched and accompanied by four familiar spirits in the shapes of an owl, a cat a snake and a crow with the forked witches' wand held high and a broomstick close to hand. Everything was centred around the cauldron, for even Shakespeare knew that without it the magic-making of the three witches would have meant nothing.

Pets, or familiars as they are known by Pagans and witches, have always been closely associated with witchcraft, whether it be in their wild or domestic state. Even monkeys have been represented as witches' attendants, for they are so akin to human beings that it is easy to see them as a spirit in human form.

Wicca has always been a mysterious religion. The details of rituals, or the names of any of the participants are never divulged to an outside party. This secrecy, witches will tell you, goes back to the days of persecution, the burning time. It is also said that retaining this information within the coven enhances perfect trust among them and that this confidentiality creates more magical power. Magical power is sustained by secrecy and is diminished when the secrecy is lost.

Top: A plaque depicting a typical interpretation of witches at work.

Above: Tea set containing zodiac signs which would be used by a witch to enhance magical powers when consulted by a client.

The traditions, rituals, spells, charms and mysticism have changed little over the years. Some hereditary witches still worship alone, but the remote village cottage has given way to the suburban semi-detached with home based altars being an important and integral part of their work. The old hag is a thing of the past, now witches are often young, attractive devotees to the craft with little or no resemblance to their olden day counterparts.

Witchcraft is still practised in many parts of Britain, and every coven has their own time-honoured tales to relate, whether they be concerned with Wiccan groups or solitary wise-women. Cornwall has always had a reputation for witchcraft, possibly due to the isolation of the county, or perhaps its abundance of sacred sites, or maybe its history which is steeped in myths, legends

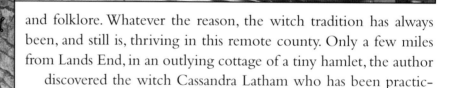

Right: A Wiccan High
Priestess
at her suburban altar.

Below: Witches'
implements.
Cauldron, witches'
ball, spirit house,
Broomstick etc.

Right:
The witch,
Cassandra
Latham.

and folklore. Whatever the reason, the witch tradition has always been, and still is, thriving in this remote county. Only a few miles from Lands End, in an outlying cottage of a tiny hamlet, the author discovered the witch Cassandra Latham who has been practicing her craft for the last 15 years. Although she originally worked within a coven, she decided many years ago to adopt a solitary path and work as a village witch using her basic principles and knowledge in a more confined environment.

Cassandra Latham is a witch with a difference. Not only does she hold the title of Wiccan Priestess, but her nursing background coupled with her healing spells have proved so successful that she has a working position in three of Cornwall's hospitals. As well as healing the sick, she uses her powers to lift curses, help people find a job or a house or give counselling and advice on the numerous problems in our everyday society. As a result of her full-time commitment, she is uniquely the first witch in history to have registered her self-employed business with the Inland Revenue!

Like so many witches she has a familiar, a cat called 'Mab' (Queen of the Fairies) who was born on the stroke of midnight, on Hallowe'en some seven years ago. Its colour has been described as moonlight, for when it is outside in the light of the moon it becomes mysteriously invisible. Initially, this cat is more ferocious than a Rotweiler, for its claws extend and it snarls aggressively at any intruder. Unless this familiar takes to you within the first ten minutes, the witch Cassandra will not tolerate your presence in her cottage.

Pets, or familiars as they are known by Pagans and witches, have always been closely associated with witchcraft, whether it be in their wild or domestic state.

Left:
The Familiar, 'Mab'.

Below left:
A 'Book of Shadows', containing details of rituals, spells, charms etc.

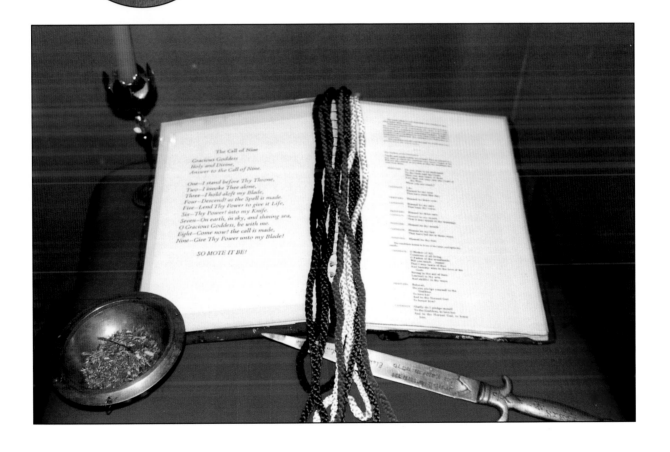

CHAPTER FOUR

SACRED SITES, RITUALS, CELEBRATIONS & INITIATIONS

To those outside Paganism and witchcraft, the ancient sites throughout the country are often just an assembly of unusually erected stones whose only appeal is in their formation and the fact that they have survived since the New Stone Age. These people might find it hard to understand why witches regard these sites as sacred, and worship there.

Witches believe that these ancestral sites contain an unseen, magical energy which is generated by the way the stones are placed. They feel an affinity to the ancient ways of our predecessors, so by performing their rituals or celebrating their festivals at these places they can be more attuned to the age-old mysteries and become closer to their Goddess and the powers of the earth. Witches use magical effectiveness as a discerning spiritual discipline. The aim of this magic is not necessarily an alteration of the outer world, but a transformation of the inner - the very spirit and soul of the witch. Through this practice, which is often referred to as High Magic, witches begin to awaken their spirit, the integral part of the soul, or psyche. This enables them to expand their consciousness and probe more deeply into nature and all its mysteries.

So many of these sacred sites are surrounded in myth. Wayland's Smithy is a 5000 year old Neolithic burial chamber in Wiltshire. Saxon settlers discovered the tomb and presumed it to be the work of one of their Gods, Wayland the Smith.

Above:
The Labyrinths
(1800 - 1400 B.C.) at
Rocky Valley near
Tintagel, Cornwall.

Left:
The Rollright Stones
(An army turned into
pillars of stone).

Above: The King Stone on the
Oxfordshire/Warwickshire border.

Above: The Whispering Knights.

A legend grew that the only way that Wayland could make a living was to shoe moorland ponies, and if you left your horse with a silver coin overnight it would be shod by morning. 1700 years after the initial construction, a further tomb was built, completely covering the first. When this was opened in 1921 it was found to have been ransacked, but the remains of eight people were found among the dishevelled pile of bones. Relics discovered near the burrows confirm that witchcraft was, and still is, practiced there.

Some sites hold more intigue for witches than others, like those with Labyrinth carvings. A witch will use these by placing her finger in the centre and, while slowly following the lines in an outward direction, summon up the energies needed to perform her magic.

The legends surrounding these sites are often bizarre and witchcraft-related. None more so than the Rollright Stones on the Oxfordshire/ Warwickshire border, for here, as at Stonehenge, Avebury and the Cheeswring of Cornwall, the all-important circular formation can be observed. This is the most important configuration to a working witch, for it is considered to be an extremely ancient symbol of community and as a circle is endless, it allows those forming that circle (as in a coven) to combine their efforts and create a cone of energy.

The legend behind the 2000 B.C. Rollright Stones is fascinating. The story tells of an ambitious king who, with his army, was marching northwards when he was confronted by a witch. She challenged him to take just seven strides and see the nearby village of Long Compton over the hill. If he could do this he would then be King of England. The king stepped forward with confidence, but a small mound hid his view. The witch declared "thou shall not be king" and turned him into stone. His army, who were assembled in one huge circle, began to laugh until they too were turned to stone. A quarter of a mile away, five knights who were whispering and plotting against the king are, to this day, still pillars of stone. The final act of the witch was to turn herself into an elder tree. When it bloomed, people would gather beside the king stone and cut into the tree. It was said that as the sap

Left:
The Hermitage and
waterfall at St Nectan's
Glen, Tintagel.

Witches who have
used this site have
described how the
atmosphere is
charged with an
extra-ordinary
peace and
tranquility. They
descend down the
waterfall into the
deep basin below,
then following the
flow of the water,
emerge through
the large hole in
the foot of the
rock, which is
considered to be
a spiritual rebirth,
and finally come
to rest in the pool
at the foot of the
rocks.

bled, the king would move his head.

One mystery still remains. It is said that it is impossible to count the stones of
the king's men, for no matter how many times you try, the number is different
on each occasion.

Many witches' sacred sites are well concealed, such as the Hermitage and waterfall at St Nectan's Glen near Tintagel, Cornwall. In order to discover this pic-
turesque sanctuary, often used during a witches' initiation, it is necessary to follow

a track through the heavily wooded glen beside the Trevillitt River on a path used
from the sixth century onwards by the pilgrims who came to pray at the shrine
of the good St Nectan. Witches who have used this site have described how the
atmosphere is charged with an extraordinary peace and tranquility. They descend
down the waterfall into the deep basin below, then following the flow of the
water, emerge through the large hole in the foot of the rock, which is considered
to be a spiritual rebirth, and finally come to rest in the pool at the foot of the rocks.

In the parish of Madron in Cornwall, the author discovered some evidence of
witches at the ruins of a Celtic church where an altar had recently been used,

Covens worship in secret, behind closed doors or at concealed locations throughout the countryside. Often these are ley centres, places where natural earth energies are powerful.

possibly at a full moon Esbat. Close by, near a sacred wishing well, customary witch tokens had been tied to a tree. This ritual, which is used by a coven at the Autumn Equinox, allows the coven member to mentally infuse the token with his or her wishes for the forthcoming year. The sheer volume of tokens which have been tied to this tree recently is some indication of the current witch population in this part of the country.

Covens worship in secret, behind closed doors or at concealed locations throughout the countryside. Often these are ley centres, places where natural earth energies are powerful.

Above left:
Incense Burner

Above right:
White Feather Fan

The altar constitutes the main focal point of all magical circles and can differ slightly from coven to coven. It is all-important that everything used and displayed on the altar is representative of the craft.

Some prefer to conduct the ceremonies naked (sky-clad). Their belief is that clothing hampers the electro-magnetic energy they intend to employ. When sky-clad, members only wear their silver rings and bracelets, as silver symbolises purity. Most witches wear loose fitting robes, usually black, and are either sandalled or barefoot.

Paganism and witchcraft are the only religions where the worshippers form a sacred circle. In other religions the person who conducts the service is a figurehead and stands out in front of the congregation. A circle has no beginning and no end, its power is that of infinity. If you take a circle and twist it in half, it becomes the sign of infinity. In the beginning and at the end there is still one, for the circle enhances all that it encompasses.

Even something as unobtrusive as the witches' hat is symbolic. The brim is an endless circle and the point of the cone represents the centre of the circle, the nucleus of power. The early church builders were also aware of this symbolism, for the majority of churches were constructed with steeples, which acted as a power centre.

The coven, which is a sacred and private undertaking, may be held almost anywhere providing that a circle, (traditionally nine feet in diameter) is cast with the black handled dagger, or athame, by an initiated couple with the rank of High Priest and High Priestess.

The consecrated athame, wand or staff can be used to cast the circle, which not only symbolises unity, but represents the circular movement of the seasons. When the circle is being cast, incense is burnt and a fan made of white feathers is used to direct this fragrance toward each participating member, an act which cleanses the mind and spirit.

The altar constitutes the main focal point of all magical circles and can differ slightly from coven to coven as some witches prefer more othodox, time-honoured altar designs. It is all-important that everything used and displayed on the altar is representative of the craft.

As witches worship the Gods of the four elements, it is an invariable practice, at an indoor ritual, to set up separate altars positioned at the four points of the compass. Each altar carefully represents one of the elements of Earth, Air, Fire or Water and homage is paid to the respective Gods in turn.

No bubbling cauldron is evident in modern witchcraft. It is seen as an outdated concept - today's witches are more concerned with spiritual attainment, which is achieved through a nature-based reverence. Even the infamous myth of thirteen member covens is outmoded. It was said that this was a parody of Christ and the twelve disciples. The fact that witchcraft existed long before Christianity makes nonsense of this idea.

Although there are eight sabbats in the witches' Calendar, outside this wheel of the year the phases of the moon, the full moon, the quarters and the waxing and waning, are all significant to ritual working practices.

These different phases all have their own relevance. The energy of a waxing moon is time for growth, whereas a waning moon is used to banish illness and unpleasantness. The inclusion of repeated chanting brings an uplifting mood to the proceedings of a coven. These, each in their own way, create a significant connection as each segment of the ritual unfolds.

Top right: The God of Fire altar.

Right: The God of Air altar.

Some are drawn to the craft because of their psychic ability, others from religious backgrounds or even a chance meeting with a witch. Whatever the circumstances may be, they tend to share a common experience, a feeling that this is their Karma.

Five different chants are repeated over and over again during a ritual.

We are the flow,
We are the ebb,
We are the witches, back from the dead,
We are the flow,
We are the ebb,
We are the weavers, we are the web.

- -

The river is flowing, growing and growing,
The river is flowing, down to the sea,
Mother Earth, carry me,
A child I will always be,
Mother Earth, carry me, down to the sea

- -

Lady spin your circle bright,
Weave your web of dark and light.
Earth, air, fire and water.
Binds us as one.

- -

Building bridges between our divisions,
I reach out for you and you reach out for me,
With all our voices, and all our visions,
Brothers we can make such a sweet harmony,
Sisters we can make such a sweet harmony,

- -

Cauldron of changes, feather on the bone,
Our arc of eternity, ring around the sun,
We are the old people, we are the new people,
We are the same people, wiser than before.

The process of becoming a witch, the way of the wise, is a hard one. Some are drawn to the craft because of their psychic ability, others from religious backgrounds or even a chance meeting with a witch. Whatever the circumstances may be, they tend to share a common experience, a feeling that this is their Karma. The would-be witch must learn the skills of the Craft and discover the areas where he or she has the most aptitude.

As no coven recruits members, many witches choose to follow the way alone, seeking to commune with nature in the fields and forests and to work solo in the ways of the Wise woman or Cunning man. This enhancement of their knowledge and spell-power is their equivalent of an apprenticeship.

Below:
A Buckinghamshire Coven.

The would-be witch must learn the skills of the Craft and discover the areas where he or she has the most aptitude.

Above: A Coven of Witches.

Above: Congregation of Pagans, Celts, Druids and Witches at Avebury, Wiltshire.

If the coven is in agreement, the initiation takes place a year and a day from the the time of the request.

Those who choose the path of the coven find that it requires persistence. It is difficult to find Craft groups or individuals as much of Wiccan practice remains secret. Many writers on witchcraft declare that a rite of self-initiation can be performed. The idea that one must be correctly initiated by a witch is more traditional. It is customary for a would-be witch to approach a coven and ask for initiation. If the coven is in agreement, the initiation takes place a year and a day from the the time of the request. This probationary period is to ensure the seriousness of the would-be witches' attitude and commitment, for witches take initiation very seriously. No coven will consider admitting anyone until they are absolutely satisfied that the individual's motives for joining are correct and that the person is right for the craft.

At the 4000 year-old Avebury stone circle in Wiltshire the Autumn Equinox (Mabon) takes place. This is the time of year when Pagans, Celts, Druids and Witches combine forces to celebrate collectively and give thanks to the God and Goddess for the crops and produce of the season past. Emma and Phillip, shamanic names Bobcat and Wolf walks with Fire, take on the respective roles of the God and Goddess. The congregation separates into two groups; the Goddess party, led by the Guardian of the Stones, makes its way to the southern entrance of the henge, where the Guardian takes her place in the western portal stone.

The other group, the God party, make their way round the perimeter of the henge in procession to be greeted by the Guardian at the southern entrance. The ceremony commences with tokens of gratitude being presented to the Guardian, the gift of flowers of the season and the significant sheaf-loaf baked from the corn of the harvest.

As the proceedings continue, the sacred circle is formed and prayers and blessings are administered, the Gods of the elements are honoured in turn and children receive a blessing. Then the sacred Sabbat ritual of Hand-fasting takes place.

Above:
The Goddess party en route to the Southern Henge at Avebury.

Left:
Gifts from the seasons.

This is a wedding and the commitment lasts for a year and a day. The partnership is only binding for this period, after which time it can be renewed at an anniversary ceremony or dissolved by mutual agreement.

Right:
'Bobcat' and 'Wolf running with Fire'

Below right:
Handfasting ceremony at the Autmn Equinox, Avebury, Wiltshire

Below left:
An incense burner used in the centre circle at large gatherings.

CHAPTER FIVE

WITCHES' EQUIPMENT

Over the years, the witches' broom has captured the imagination far more effectively than any other piece of magical equipment. In folklore the broom is the primary means of travel for witches and the witch riding her broomstick has become a universal stereotype.

The image of this bound bundle of twigs sweeping her tracks from the sky has persisted into the 20th century. The origin of this is unclear. Prior to the late 17th century, it was considered that a witch rode her broomstick with the brush end lower and at the rear. This is probably an association with the times when

Pagans performed fertility rites to encourage crop growth. They were known to mount brooms, pichforks and poles and ride them like hobbyhorses into the fields, while dancing and leaping in the air. As witches were credited for their powers of flight above their other accomplishments, the flying crone is an enduring image.

At the end of the 17th century the portrayals of the witch showed her using her accepted form of transport differently. Now she was depicted flying her broom to the sabbat with the brush end up and in front, sometimes with a candle in the brush to light her way, and accompanied by her familiar -

Right:
The Besom or Witches' Broom.

Below:
Witches raising a storm at sea
(Olaus Magnus, Historia de gentibus septentrionalibus, 1555).

a black cat. It was a popular belief that after the sabbat, witches would fly out to sea and empty the contents of their obnoxious cauldrons into the water which would raise storms and tempests.

Some believed that the Devil gave every newly initiated witch flying ointment and a broom. A variation of this belief stated that he dispensed these items only to weak witches who needed help. Before setting off on their broomsticks, witches had to anoint themselves with the flying ointment, which consisted of a vile concoction of hallucinogenic drugs that disordered their senses and gave the the illusion of flight.

The fact that they were inside a house was of little consequence, for they supposedly rose up through the chimney and took flight. In medieval times the belief that witches travelled on brooms was more widespread in the rest of Europe than in England. Today the besom broom still retains its importance in the craft. It takes pride of place at the altar, where in a coven a High Priestess uses it to symbolically sweep away evil when clearing the space for a magic circle.

All witches' tools are of great personal significance and cannot be shared. It is generally agreed upon that the witches' equipment must be handmade and, once consecrated, never used for any other purpose. The idea behind this teaching is that, with time, they become infused with the user's vibrations and take on magical properties for the user. The process of consecration involves the use of sea salt and holy water, the latter obtained from sacred and ancient wells or springs. When mixed, they are blessed in the name of the God and the Goddess, the combination of these acts as a cleansing and purifying agent and dedicates the equipment to the divine.

Top: The North Berwick coven 1591: members drink in a cellar, another takes down the words of the Devil preaching from a pulpit, others boil up a cauldron to create a storm and sink a ship at sea.

Above: Witches flying up a chimney on broomsticks (Thomas Erastus, Dialogues touchant le pouvoir des sorcièrers et la puniton qu'elles meritent, 1579).

The moon is the
source of the
witch's power,
drawn down from
the sky; it is the
worker of Magic.
Even though man
has set foot on the
moon it still retains
its mystery,
because of its
association with
the tides and
phases. The Craft
believes it also has
an affinity with
silver and the
enigma of the
number seven.

Concocting flying
ointment before the
Sabbat(Hans Baldung
Grien, 1513).

Should it be a clear, starry night when this ceremony is being performed
then tools are laid on a windowsill so they can be bathed in the rays of the sil-
very moon. The moon is the source of the witch's power, drawn down from
the sky; it is the worker of Magic. Even though man has set foot on the moon

it still retains its mystery, because of its association with the tides and phases. The Craft believes it also has an affinity with silver and the enigma of the number seven. This is enhanced by the fact that silver is made up of seven elements; there are seven seas; seven colours in the rainbow and seven days in the week. This precious metal, with all its associations, is so revered that witches' jewellery, together with the majority of their metallic working tools, incorporates as much silver as possible.

In witchcraft the magic circle provides a sacred and sanctified perimeter in which all rituals, magical work and worship are conducted. It symbolises completion and unity, the cycle of the seasons and birth-death regeneration. When the circle has been cast, coveners are invited inside through a spiritual gate, which is then closed. The circle itself then becomes a consecrated area, a magical focus for the four elements.

The sacred black-handled athame, with its carved

Above: Ceremonial Sword.

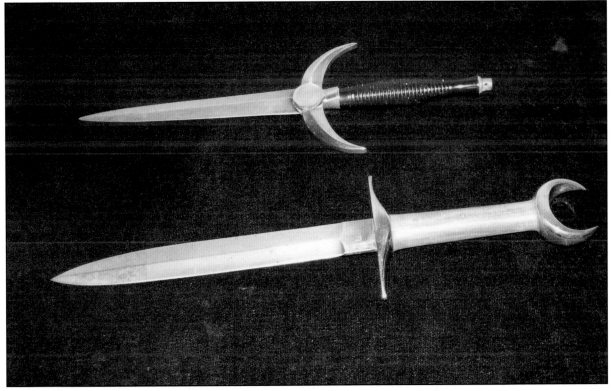

Above: Ritual Athames

Above:
Chalices used for sacred water or wine.

magical symbols, becomes an extension of one's inner self and is known as the witches' knife. This is traditionally used for casting a circle, but the consecrated wand, staff or sword can also be used for this purpose.

These days, wands can be aquired made from natural materials ranging from wood to crystal. Wands made from a living tree are thought to be permeated with great spiritual power. A wand fashioned from willow is believed to be a wand of water, moon and enchantment, but if a spell requires the banishing of negativity then blackthorn would be used. When acquiring a wand from a tree, a straight and slender branch is selected, it is then hollowed at the centre, sanded smooth, filled with cotton wool, then brought to life with three drops of the witches own blood.

When the circle is cast the athame is returned to its rightful position on the altar. The altar is a complex and meaningful place of devotion. Everything on the altar is representational and must be displayed according to its respective balance. When a covener faces the sacred altar they are neither black nor white, but in an intermediate position between the two. White and black are represented on an altar by the right and left sides repectively. Flowers, in the form of foxcloves and belladonna (deadly nightshade) corresponding to the good and bad in nature, can also be used to depict the two extremes. The all-important figure or symbol representing the Goddess takes pride of place at the centre of the altar. The Stang, a four-forked staff, symbolises her consort with the antlered Horned God. The High Priestess and Priest personify these positions within a coven. The four elements can be represented by a pentacle (earth), an incense burner (air), a dish of water (water) and a candle (fire).

Other altar arrangemnts may include a sword, a skull, an altar-cloth and a white-handled knife. A cauldron and a besom broom are placed either side of the altar.

Each of these witches' tools represents the workings of the coven in its own particular way. Today the burning of those early tallow candles has been replaced by coloured wax candles of black, white, red, blue or green which assist in spells, for colour plays an important part in magic, with each colour having its own association. Black (negativity), white (love and peace), red (relationships), blue (protection) and green (abundance).

Some witches believe that the use of an elaborately furnished altar with silver chalices, candlesticks and incense thuribles shows an appropriate reverence to the Goddess. Others think that this type of display contravenes the craft tradition which attaches little meaning to material wealth. Most witches are proud of their altars and do their utmost to have them beautifully presented. It takes many years of devotion and dedication to become a High Priest or Priestess.

Above:
High Priest
Reg Griffiths.

Witchcraft is made up of a variety of different phenomena, most of which extend beyond the boundaries of normal comprehension. Because it involves mystical practices which are unusual to an outsider, it is suspect and becomes subject to that ancient predjudice which says 'What takes place illogically must be evil and therefore destroyed.' A devotee to the craft is presumed to work the thin line between good and evil. That is why, even in modern society, the word 'witch' is still feared.

Little has been done, over the years, to change this image, for witchcraft is continually receiving bad press. Not for what they are doing but for what they are said to have done in the past.

Today's witches are highly individualistic and can be found in almost all walks of life. Unfortunately, as witchcraft is not an openly publicised religion, it is criticised incessantly, although witches naturally defend their religion,

their beliefs and their participation. Considering the adverse publicity that witchcraft receives, it is not a path for the faint-hearted to follow. Total commitment and allegiance to the craft is uppermost to a witch .

As previously mentioned, covens take great pride in fashioning their altars, yet this is not considered essential. No set rules are laid down within the craft as to the appearance of an altar, only that the tools used should be significantly representational. The altar is mainly a focal point for the ritual, the place where the 'working tools' are positioned. Such is the devotion of a hedge witch, or witches that have chosen to work alone, that their altar may be a simple table or a wooden box standing on bricks indoors. If a ceremony takes place outside, rocks or tree stumps may be adopted for the purpose of an altar. Whatever construction is used, it should not contain conductive materials, such as iron or steel, since they can interfere with the energy of ritual tools. In witchcraft, procedures can be followed but rules of worship are flexible. Once the cone of power has been invoked, through the Goddess, those present

Above: This is the trunk of a west country working witch who got by in her craft with the minimum amount of gear. What she needed could be safely housed and treasured in a small travelling trunk. This was once the property of Molly Adams of Taunton, Somerset. These trunks were kept under a witches' bed and were a size that could travel on horseback, mail coach or carter's dray. Tradition and usage dictated that they be small, that is why in so many witchcraft operations it is the client who is instructed to go out and purchase, find or steal the necessary items required by the witch for her to concoct her charms and spells.

can concentrate on the work to be done This is the time when wishes, hopes and dreams, for yourself and others, are conveyed through the use of magic.

Hypnosis has been a Wiccan skill for centuries. To practice this, witches have always used the 'Witches Ball'. These reflective glass balls were manufactured by Nailsea glass-makers from 1788 onwards. They are about seven inches in diameter and usually coloured blue or green. Some were even silvered or decorated in elaborate swirling patterns. They were dangled in front of the subject to induce the hypnotic state, in the same way that a variety of other bright objects have been similarly used. The witches' ball is also used as a charm, it is

In witchcraft, procedures can be followed but rules of worship are flexible. Once the cone of power has been invoked, through the Goddess, those present can concentrate on the work to be done

Hypnosis has been
a Wiccan skill for
centuries. To
practice this,
witches have
always used the
'Witches Ball'.
These reflective
glass balls are
about seven inches
in diameter and
usually coloured
blue or green.

suspended in a window or dark corner of a house, where it will reflect evil and ill-fortune.

It should be constantly kept clean in order that the ball can attract ill-luck and ill-wishing that would otherwise have fallen on the household. As in all crafts, the tools of the witches' trade are employed for a specific purpose. The Chalice is a container for wine or water. The witch wears a magical Binding Cord around her waist. The Charm Bag is occasionally worn round the neck. The Necklaces and Rings are believed to have magical properties. The Book Of Shadows contains spells and charms.

Last, but not least, the most prolific and commonly associated item of a witches' inventory is the Cauldron. This is the three-legged

cooking pot of olden days and the great provider of sustenance. It has become symbolic as its fat-bellied shape is an image of womanhood and fertility and the three legs remind one of the Triple Goddess. It is a utensil with a macabre history, in which magical brews, potions and spells were concocted for good or evil!

Left: Witches stirring up a brew in a cauldron.

Below Left: Witches brewing magical potions.

The Cauldron. is the three-legged cooking pot of olden days and the great provider of sustenance. It has become symbolic as its fat-bellied shape is an image of womanhood and fertility and the three legs remind one of the Triple Goddess.

Above:
The Hedge witches'
ingredients.

CHAPTER SIX

SPELLS, CHARMS, CURES, MAGIC AND HEALING

Witches definitely cast spells, either alone or in covens. It is a spoken or written magical formula that is designed to change or influence a particular course of events. Spells have a close resemblance to prayer, a ritual which consists of a request to a deity for the purpose of a desired outcome.

Spell-casting is usually carried out at the Esbats, the lunar festivals. Witches believe that the moon influences our psyche and that they are more magically powerful at the full moon. It is also maintained that the hour of midnight is important, as this is the time when those powers are at their greatest peak, enabling magical strength to be drawn down. Subsequently, this time has always been known as the 'Witching Hour'.

For spells to be effective they must be of original composition or based on successful formulae handed down by spell-casters of the past. They may be beneficial or harmful, and they work on both man and beast. When a witch is proficient in her craft she has the capability to work both extremes of evil and good. The wise-woman of old was to be repected or avoided, for invoking her displeasure could result in extremely unfortunate consequences.

In the past, malignant witches gained a reputation for cursing and were responsible for ruining crops, extreme weather conditions, bringing death upon herds of cattle, causing conflict between husband and wife and bringing about misery and suffering to those who had courted their displeasure. These are not fables but actual malevolent acts brought about by the witch with her 'evil eye'.

Even the casting of spells, which is widely different from the act of cursing, has always been considered a dark, occult practice, mainly because it operates outside the realms of rational everyday understanding. There are a limitless variety of spells. These can include spells for success, fertility, protection from disaster, ill fortune or evil, important decisions, love and health. The

Above: Spell Jar. A thorn piercing the animal's tongue and kidney. This refers to the animal's owner, the farmer. The next stage would have been to place these items in a miniature grave close to the offending farmer's house where they would rot away, giving this revengeful spell time to work its magic.

method used by a witch brings about a change in people's everyday life, it affects their moods, their attitudes and conscious ways of thought. This is achieved through the administration of potions and spiritual thought transference. From time immemorial, witches have been herbalists, the apothecaries to their communities, who concoct medicines from plants and hedgerows.

However, their reputation invariably suffered when a cure was ineffective for then they were often labelled as poisoners or charlatans.

Today the power of the witch is as strong as it has ever been. The main dif-

Right: Birds in a nest. Flying plays a vital role in the world of magic, birds have the power of natural flight, denied to man. With a few flaps of their wings they are up, off and away. Birds were seen as the messengers between heaven and the earth below. Here we have a blue and white plate, blue of sky and white of cloud and a birds nest, which equals earth house and home, and four dead bird skulls. This means trouble for some local household and four persons who have a problem between them. This spell was discovered in a sealed off roof section of an old cottage.

Right:
The Hedgerow.

ference being that now her energies are more positively directed. Recently a charity contacted a Wiccan High Priestess and asked if she could ensure that the weather would be fine for their fête, the following Saturday. On the afternoon in question, dark storm clouds hung heavily over the area, promising to ruin the event. The witch Madam Morgana described how, after mentally placing her guardians around her, she contacted the God and Goddess for the energy needed to perform this spell. Finding a chink of blue sky in the dark-

Today the power of the witch is as strong as it has ever been. The main difference being that now her energies are more positively directed. Recently a charity contacted a Wiccan High Priestess and asked if she could ensure that the weather would be fine for their fète, the following Saturday.

Spellbound by
Peter E. Pracownik.

ening clouds, she concentrated on that tiny area, sending out prayers to disperse the clouds. Then, working from an easterly direction in a clockwise rotation, she began to push her power up towards that tiny section of blue sky, asking for the clouds to be redirected twenty miles away in case there were crops that needed the rain there. Slowly the section of blue sky became larger until eventually the sky above the area became cloudless. Needless to say, the fète was a success and funds were raised for a worthwile cause.

The use of a poppet, made of clay, wax or cloth, has always been associated with witchcraft. Often mistakenly referred to as 'Devil Dolls', they have been ritually and magically used for many different purposes, ranging from the piercing of these figures to cause death or disease to the compassionate magic called upon to bring lovers together.

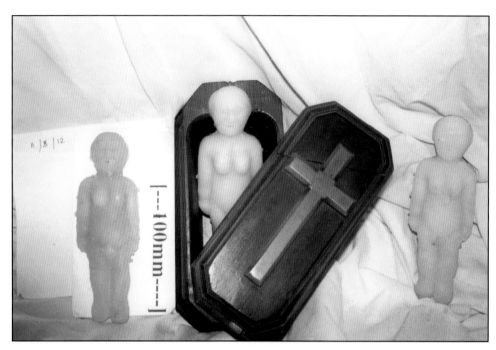

Above: Poppets with a sinister purpose. Everyone should take a little interest in coffins. We will all make use of them, one day. Certainly witches know all about their aspects and usage. This is a puzzle sarcophagus made of various woods. The trick is discovering how it can be re-opened once it is closed. Within it are wax doll poppets. Each one has a slot in its back in which written spells, nail clippings, hair etc. can be inserted before closing the coffin. This is straightforward ill-wishing black magic.

Some spells are more complex than others and require effigies of the person that the spell is being cast upon. The use of a poppet, made of clay, wax or cloth, has always been associated with witchcraft. Often mistakenly referred to as 'Devil Dolls', they have been ritually and magically used for many different purposes, ranging from the piercing of these figures to cause death or disease to the compassionate magic called upon to bring lovers together. In order to represent the recipient the doll is fashioned in their likeness and sometimes a personal effect, such as a strand of hair, is added to substantiate the link between them and thus increase the power of the spell. Medieval witches were said to throw bent pins into their cauldrons of bubbling brew to either cast or break evil spells.

Pins were also used for the spell of blessing a friend with happiness and prosperity. The ritual required the witch to pick a lemon at midnight and, while reciting the appropriate chant, stick pins of various bright colours into the lemon. If, however, the spell was needed to curse an enemy, the same procedure was adopted but this time the pins would have black heads.

In neo-pagan witchcraft less emphasis is placed on the precision of words in spells and more on the power and desire that go into the ritual to make it work. Spell-casting, whether it be done by a coven or an individual witch, is carried out within the magic circle or a protected, consecrated space.

In order to draw down the energies needed when working alone, a solitary witch will sometimes use a pair of bullroarers. When these are spun in the air above the head they emit a strange, whirring sound. Their purpose is to create an energy field that the witch can work within. A good example of these these bullroarers at work can be seen in the film Crocodile Dundee II.

Not many spells are instantaneous, many need patience to bring them to fruition and it is often many months before the desired result is accomplished. A far cry from that immortal culinary preparation from 'Macbeth': *Double, double, toil and trouble;…Fire burn and cauldron bubble…Fillet of a fenny snak…in the cauldron boil and bake.*

There is no evidence that magical spells conducted by a solo or hedge witch are any less powerful than a coven even though a greater 'cone' of energy is raised by a coven as a result of the numbers present.

Like so many writers on witchcraft, I too have fallen into the trap of categorising all witches as female, but in modern witchcraft there are equal numbers of men and women. I find it a difficult habit to break, so to those Witches, Cunning Men and High Priests out there, please do not reach for your book of spells. I do not relish the thought of being turned into a toad, so please accept my sincere apologies.

Left: Naked poppet with pins through the heart. This was an office affair…so often the cause of trouble, which led eventually to the wife asking the local witch to put a stop to it. Two pins pierce the heart and breast of the blonde. The doll is naked, indicating the temptation of her flesh, the ankles are firmly bound to keep her legs together…Need one say more? Yes, through the witch, the wife won the day…the romance was over!

Energy. By
Peter E. Pracownik.

While on the subject of toads....A witches familiar usually assumed animal form, the toad being a legendary favourite. This animal was most revered by witches for they considered that under that rough, ugly exterior there beats a heart full of affection for anyone who cares to treat and talk with them, and show love, compassion and respect.

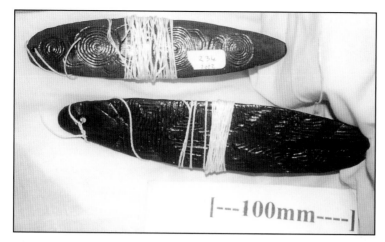

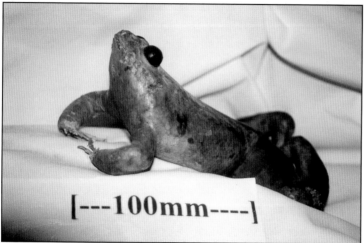

The witches discovered this fact of nature centuries ago, that showing kindness to ugly and repellent human beings and animals brings rich rewards to the giver of affection. These lovable, magical creatures have the fairy power to bring in rich rewards. So be warned!....Be kind to toads.

One of the prime functions of a spell is to ward off evil spirits and protect dwellings. Spells and charms come in various shapes and sizes, from the talisman constructed from horse hair (or garlic) and ribbons, the ribbons representing the colours of the four elements, to the 'Witches' Bottle'.

Into the Witches' Bottle must go pieces of broken glass, pottery, nails, in fact anything sharp. Then it must be urinated into, before being buried under the lintel of the house, the doorstep, or bricked-up in a fireplace. This house-cleansing, or banishing, is sometimes necessary to deal with irregularities caused by echoes of the past remaining in a dwelling. The property may feel unfriendly, or cause depression and unrest. A long-empty house becomes unwell, needing the love and warmth of occupants.

One spell, which can be performed by anyone, consists of visiting every

Top left: Bullroarers.

Lowerleft: Toad.

Above right: Horse Hair and ribbons.

One of the prime functions of a spell is to ward off evil spirits and protect dwellings.

room and opening all the cupboards. Then with a calm, comforting, sincere and positive mental approach, demand the dismissal of any negative energy by emitting your own loving personality and gratitude towards a happy liason with the occupiers and the property.

Witches profess that some spells are easy and that they can be performed by anyone, provided that the correct mental approach is adopted and that the spell is not directed against a fellow human being, for this is believed to come back on you with threefold repercussions.

Cord Magic is a very old way of working. Pictures from the middle ages show witches selling knotted cord to sailors. The belief was that the witches were supposed to have tied the wind up in the knots, so if a sailor needed to

Right:
Bumble bees and pouch. The pouch containing the bees was found in the corner of a room in a cottage. This was used for the purpose of attracting sunshine.

One spell, which can be performed by anyone, consists of visiting every room and opening all cupboards. Then with a calm, comforting, sincere and positive mental approach, demand the dismissal of any negative energy by emitting your own loving personality and gratitude towards a happy liason with the occupiers and the property.

Above: Witches' Bottle for house cleansing

call up the wind to fill his sails, he simply untied as many knots as necessary. The magic of the cord can be used for spell-casting in many different ways, provided the mind is quite clear about the purpose of the spell. Magic should only be used for important things, rather than for a fanciful whim.

If you feel so inclined, try this cord magic for yourself. You will need a piece of cord, three feet long. The length is important because the figure three is a magical number. Where possible, use a cord whose particular colour appeals to you. It is best to perform this spell at midnight, alone in a room lit only by candles and a favorite incense burning to create an ideal atmosphere. When quite ready, light the candles and prepare the incense. Then sit quietly for a few moments thinking about the spell. Consider the 'for and against' and the way in which it will improve your life and make you happier. With a clear mind, void of all other thoughts, believe in what you are doing, for belief gives the spell power. Pass the cord through the heat of the candle and the fragrance of the incense several times, while whispering the words of your wish. Then begin to tie the knots in the right order. First tie a knot at the end of the cord, then tie a knot at the other end. The third knot should be in the middle, and the fourth and fifth half-way between each end and the middle, then a knot half-way between each of these. This will leave nine evenly-spaced knots.

This is the pattern of the knots with the words that should be said as you tie each one.

By the knot of one the spell's begun

1 --

By the knot of two it cometh true

x ---2

By the knot of three thus it shall be

x------------------------------- 3 ----------------------------- x

By the knot of four it's strengthened more

x--------------------- 4 --------------------- x ---------------------x

By the knot of five the spell shall thrive

x --------------- x --------------- x --------------- 5 ---------------x

By the knot of six this spell I fix

x ----------- 6 ----------- x ----------- x ----------- x ----------- x

By the knot of seven the stars of heaven

x --------- x ---------- x ---------- 7 ---------- x ---------- x -------- x

By the knot of eight the hand of fate

x ------- x ------- x ------- x ------- x ------- 8 -------- x -------- x

By the knot of nine what's done is mine

x-------x-------x-------x-------x-------x-------x------9-------x

After the last knot has been tied, you again pass the cord through the fragrance of the incense. Extinguish the candles and go straight to bed, putting the cord under your pillow. While you are waiting for the result of your spell, leave the cord at home in a safe place and do not tell anyone, as this sort of

West country spirit houses have their bases filled with items of a symbolic meaning, such as stones, grit, feathers, eggshells and personal items. Should you come across one, my advice is to leave well alone, just smile and say "All rather quaint, isn't it?" and then move on.

magic works best if kept secret. When you feel sure that your spell has worked and all is going well or, for various reasons, it becomes clear that your wish is simply not going to come true, all you need to do is burn the cord and scatter or bury the ashes. Don't forget, not everyone gets what they ask for, but when your spells work, be sure to say "Thank you".

Spirit houses often have their bases filled with items of a symbolic meaning, such as stones, grit, feathers, eggshells and personal items. A great deal of folklore knowledge and an understanding of the world of spirit force is called upon when using these items. Should you come across one, my advice is to leave well alone.

The art of poppet-making and using these effigies to achieve magical intentions can be traced back to the dawn of time, when mankind developed a reasoning mind. Their successful employment has been, and always will be, invaluable to the magical art of spell-casting.

Today we live in a high-tech age and even witches have to keep abreast of the times, so occasionally they make use of photographic images in place of

Don't forget, not everyone gets what they ask for, but when your spells work, be sure to say "Thank you".

their traditional poppets of wax or clay. The most popular method employed to hurt a victim is to slowly burn a photograph of the victim, or cause it to smoulder at the edges by gently blowing upon it. An example of this is the 'wronged wife' scenario - twentieth century ill-wishing, or a case of 'Leave my husband alone'!

Tittle-tattle is the scouge of community, no matter where. The spell that witches use to deal with scandal-mongers is to acquire a personal item of material from the victim, fashion this into a face, then a nice sharp needle or pin is stuck through the false tongue. This usually puts an end to the gossip.

The power of the mind should never be underestimated, for when it is coupled with a powerful emotion such as revenge, it can unleash a dangerous weapon, as an A.T.S. sergeant found out during World War II. She was a 'Grade A bitch' who came down hard on the youngsters in her unit once too often. So, to even the score, they knotted quite a spell in the hope that their tyrant of a sergeant would really 'get knotted'. The spell worked, for the poor woman went out of her mind.

Love spells can be a nightmare for the working witch. Her clients expect her to find them a partner, cause desire in a woman, make them attractive to the opposite

Right: A blonde doll poppet with a knife through the side. Women have a dangerous knack of becoming pregnant by the wrong man. As anyone knows, this can cause trouble...it always has done and still does, as any witch can testify. One way out of this is for her to call up and make use of 'Get-rid-of magic'. This doll with the dagger in her stomach is the solution of one such case.

Below right: 'Doll Face'.

Above: A.T.S. Poppet.　　　　　　Above: Poppet of a pregnant nurse.

sex, have their feelings reciprocated by someone that they have just met and even break the bonds of love between partners. The witch has to use her discretion before she enters into her spell-casting, in case she is extending the bounds of her match-making and bringing together couples who already have a legal partner. This can result in wrecking a family especially if a third party becomes pregnant, which was the case of a nurse who consulted a witch when she found out that she was 'in trouble'. The same old story...too much to drink on a Saturday night...from sex to sadness, worry and fear, culminating in an act of witchcraft designed to cause a miscarriage. The witch, who was consulted in 1941, used a spell in conjunction with a poppet fashioned as the nurse. She pushed a stake into the poppet's stomach, destroying any form of life that might have begun.

Love spells can be a nightmare for the working witch. Her clients expect her to find them a partner, cause desire ... and even break the bonds of love between partners.

CHAPTER SEVEN

SCRYING AND DIVINATION

Above: The life-lines of the palm. On every hand the line of destiny is written.

Top: What does the future hold? Madam Morgana of the house of Avalon.

An insatiable desire to know what the future holds has always been an integral part of human nature. We all want to see what lies ahead. Gypsies, along with witches, have been renowned practitioners of the occult and have had a profound influence on the development of folk magic. The mystery of the gypsy sitting in her booth attracts like a magnet when she utters those immortal words, "Cross my palm with silver and I will tell your future."

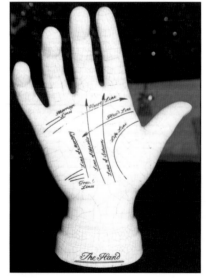

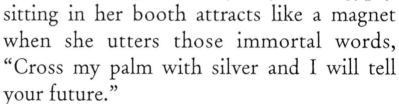

This gypsy has become the stereotypical version, a woman fortune-teller who gazes into a crystal ball or knowingly studies the lines and contours on the palm of your hand, creating that all-important ambience of mystery in her dimly lit surroundings. Contrary to popular belief, the cryptic atmosphere at a reading is not part of some theatrical pretence but a necessary setting.

Above: Scrying. Using a crystal ball to look into the future.

Palmistry has a close connection to astrology. Long ago someone named the parts of the hand after the planets. In palmistry, the 'arrangement' of a planet is decided by the texture, pattern and length of a particular part of the hand. The reader's predictions are based on the unique configiration of the palm, for, like fingerprints, no two hands are the same.

The form of prediction known as Scrying is an ancient art in which clairvoyance is achieved by concentrating upon an object with a shiny surface. The term scrying comes from the english word *descry*, which means "to make out faintly', or to reveal. The art of scrying and divination has been documented since Roman times when that anonymous soothsayer warned Caesar about the fall of Rome. The use of a crystal ball is the most popular method of scrying - the concentration upon a shiny surface until visions appear. Witches say that during this time they are working with pure energy, which is in their bodies and around them, as if they are a magnet which can draw the energy they need to complete the operation. They consider that the images received come through their 'third eye' vision.

This particular form of divination is not only limited to crystal balls, or witch balls, which are mounted on a stand, but can be achieved with virtu-

Above: A consultation with a witch in her cottage.

Above: Looking into the future through a reflective or darkened mirror.

ally any shiny or smooth surface that makes a good reflector.

The ancient Egyptians were known to use ink, blood and other dark liquids in containers when scrying. This principle has changed little over the years, for even to this day witches use a cauldron or dark vessel filled with water or gaze into a mirror, whether it be the reflective or the darkened variety, to obtain their clairvoyant spiritual communication.

The accuracy of many prophets, seers, crystal-gazers and fortune tellers has been recorded throughout history. None more so than that French healer, astrologer and prophet Nostradamus who, among other things, predicted the French Revolution; the rise and fall of Napoleon; the rise of Hitler (400 years before World War II) and the assassinations of both the Kennedy brothers. Nostradamus, who was a skilled reader of horoscopes, used a combination of astrological references and an astonishing visionary gift to generate his meticulous predictions. He also used bowls of water to see the visions from which he produced his celebrated prophecies. Every culture has had its soothsayers who were either revered and respected or despised and feared, as was the wrinkled old wise woman in that isolated cottage, who could foretell the future with such uncanny perception.

Both scrying and divination are an integral part of witchcraft. This means that witches look closely at people through various predicting instruments such as crystal balls, Tarot cards and rune stones.

Because witches use the power of their mind, they obtain vibrations from the clients who come to them for advice. This enables them, through their subconscious, to receive from high level spiritual counsellors, clairvoyant visions of objects, events, places and people. This method is similar to psychometry, that ultrasensitive ability that allows the practitioner to 'read' a personality from personal items such as clothing, jewellery or even correspondence sealed inside an envelope. Although scrying is simply defined as gazing into a reflective surface, this is only the beginning of the process. After a while the subconscious moves into a channelling state, thereby opening up the psyche, which is considered to be influenced by the phases of the moon. Clairvoyance is an extrasensory perception (ESP) which is accombination of precognition (knowledge of the future) and telepathy. It is sometimes known as second sight, whereas astrology and palmistry are more scientific divination methods. Second sight or 'the Gift' as it was referred to in the old days, was considered a special talent possessed by a selected few. Everyday we regularly use our five senses of sight, touch, hearing, smell and taste, but it has long been maintained that human beings have a sixth sense which is totally independent of the other five. It is now known that all people

Above: The cards disclose their secrets.

Left:
The Pentagram...
a magic symbol.

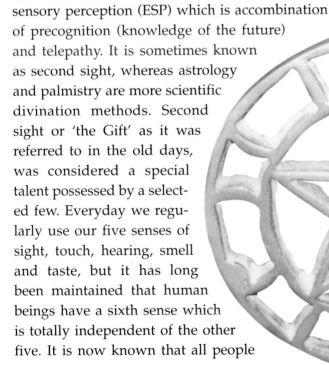

Right:
Ancient Tarot deck.

Below: The ominous
death card.

have this ability in varying degrees. In the past, when people lived closer to nature and their minds were not over-stressed by the fast pace of modern life, these powers would develop more easily.

Witches believe that we are all caught up in a never-ending life process. They consider that we exist eternally and that death is not an ending but merely a beginning - a gateway, without heaven or hell, to a new life through reincarnation. They say that our path of destiny is mapped out for us from the day we are born and although we have freedom of choice and invariably, through misplaced decisions, stray off the path down avenues of uncertainty, we will always return to our inescapable fate and follow life's intended course. What will be, will be.

Although scrying and divination can be loosely defined as fortune-telling, this definition is inappropriate, for the magical word 'fortune' is the grail of our hopes, our belief that money is the answer to all our problems. We only have to look at the hundreds of millionaires that lotteries have created and the instantaneous change to their lives, which has not always been as idyllic as their dreams. Even money brings problems, whether it be friends who no longer feel worthy or the loss of incentive and motivation to work.

Tarot cards have always been synonymous with witchcraft. This does not mean that every Tarot reader is a witch. In fact, many competent readers use their gift entirely outside any religious convictions they may have. It is possible that the proficient combination of scrying and divination techniques within their craft determines the witch.

The Tarot is an oracle, a means for divining the future, but it will also give an insight into the past and present. The true age of the Tarot is unknown, even though several theories have been put forward to explain its origin. We do know that the Tarot is closely linked with our modern playing cards which are believed to have originated in China, as far back as the 11th century.

There are 78 cards in the Tarot deck, which are divided into two sections: The Major Arcana, or 'Trumps' and the Minor Arcana with its four suits: Batons (fire), Swords (air), Cups (water), and Coins (earth) - each suit corresponds to one of the four elements. In a Tarot reading, each card represents a facet in one's past, present and future life.

Once the cards are shuffled by the client, who is believed to impregnate them with his or her individual magnetism, they are placed face-down in a ten card configuration. The client is known as the questioner. He or she sits facing the reader with a mind cleared of all thoughts except those relevant to the reading taking place. The first six cards only are turned face up and each card, which has only appeared through fate or chance, is interpreted according to a

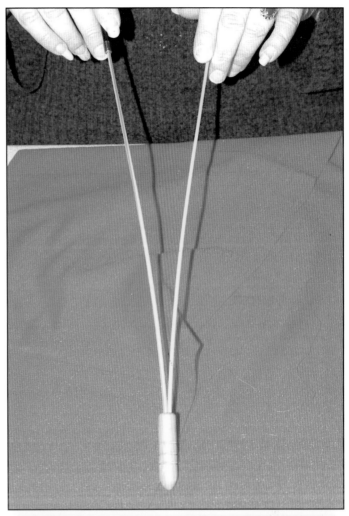

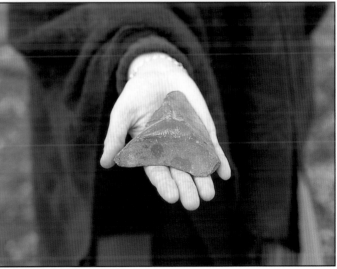

Above: Divining and dowsing rods and stones.

Many proficient
witches adopt
unorthodox
methods for
divination, using
shells, stones, or
even chicken
bones.

particular aspect of the reading:

1 - Present Position (Karma);

2 - Immediate influence; 3 - Goal or Destiny; 4 - Distant Past Foundation;

5 - Recent Past Events; 6 - Future influence.

After the reading of these six cards has been completed, the reader proceeds to turn over the remaining four cards from left to right and, working with the influences that have been revealed by the previous cards, proceeds towards an overall conclusion, a final result of the reading. When the Death card appears in a spread, the client usually thinks the worst. Surprisingly, this is not an evil omen or the prediction of a fatality, only an indication of an ending or a new beginning - the completion of a project or a phase in one's life. The art of Tarot reading has an amazing reputation for accuracy, even though the word 'Arcana' means mysteries or secrets.

Many proficient witches adopt unorthodox methods for divination, using shells, stones, or even chicken bones. These are shuffled in the hand before being cast onto a surface. The direction in which these objects point and the pattern created can tell a witch much about her client.

There are many different forms of divination. Minerals, or water beneath the ground, can be discovered by the use of dowsing rods or a crystal pendulum. This is another example of an intuitive flash, resulting from a

When using the Runes for divination, the twenty-four pieces with symbols and the blank twenty-fifth are scattered face down on the table. Shuffling is done by pushing the stones toward the client who is asked to form these into a circle, leaving one stone in the middle, which represents him or her.

Stonehenge by
Peter E. Pracownik.

psychic understanding in the subconscious, being directed through an instrument. As witchcraft is often defined as the oldest religion, its beliefs in, and connections with, the past are all-important. Witches practice ancient methods of divination because they are a respectful link with that past.

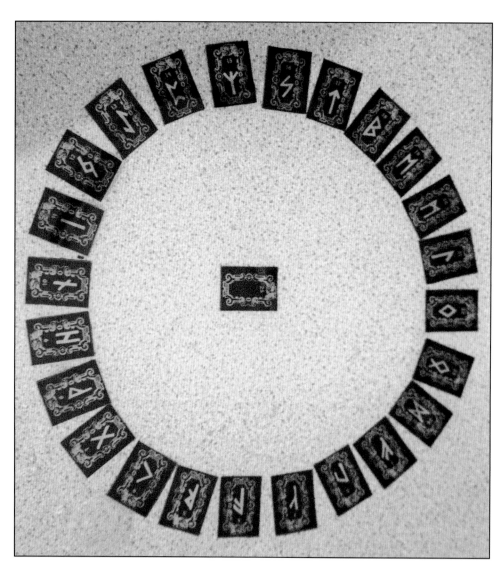

The use of Rune Stones is another ancient way of divining the future. It is
a magical alphabet of symbols used for healing, divination, charms and
spell-casting. The origin of the Runes has always been shrouded in mystery.
Historians have a more prosaic explanation for the existence of the Runes:
some say that they were developed from an original picture-alphabet similar to the hieroglyphic writings found in Egyptian tombs which was
devised by holy men or priests.

Whatever historians may say, witches recognise two meanings: firstly, that
the word 'rune' refers to a rhyme or chant which is recited during a ritual
dedicated to the forces of nature, the sun, moon and the Gods and
Goddesses. Secondly as a letter or sign, painted, carved or imprinted on a
piece of stone or wood, which is part of a magical alphabet. Proof that these
symbols stem from an old religion is confirmed by the Runic writing etched

deep into the giant pillars of Stonehenge, one of the most sacred of all the ancient temples.

When using the Runes for divination, the twenty-four pieces with symbols and the blank twenty-fifth are scattered face down on the table. Shuffling is done by pushing the stones toward the client who is asked to form these into a circle, leaving one stone in the middle, which represents him or her. As in the Tarot, each Runestone symbol is interpreted in terms of the client's past, present and future. It must not be overlooked that spells can be performed using these stones, and like all magic, they can be either good or evil. The end result, as in all spells, depends on the capabilities of the witch concerned.

Below: Crystal pendulum used for divining, dowsing and spiritual communication.

A CHANT PERFORMED DURING A RITUAL AT IMBOLC

Hail reign a fair maid,

With gold on your toe,

Open up the west gate,

And let the old year go.

- - - - - - -

Hail reign a fair maid,

With gold upon your chin,

Open up the east gate;

And let the New Year in.

Rejoice, sing rejoice,

The water and the wine,

The seven bright gold wires,

And the candles that do shine.

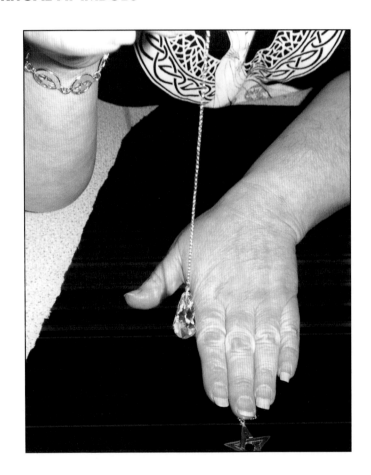

As in the Tarot, each Runestone symbol is interpreted in terms of the client's past, present and future. It must not be overlooked that spells can be performed using these stones, and like all magic, they can be either good or evil. The end result, as in all spells, depends on the capabilities of the witch concerned.

CHAPTER EIGHT
WITCH-HUNTS AND PERSECUTIONS

Hopkins, the witch finder.

The 'Burning Time' is a term used by neo-Pagan witches to refer to the period of western history from the mid-15th to the early 18th centuries, a period of intense witch-hunting and executions. Not all witches were burned at the stake: hanging was the preferred means of execution in England and the American colonies.

In England the worst time of persecution for witches was the 17th century under the auspicious direction of Matthew Hopkins who gained the infamous title of 'Witchfinder Generall' for the barbaric methods he used to obtain confessions.

Hopkins is believed to have been born in Manningtree, Essex in 1620. In those days, Manningtree was considered a sizeable market town and one of the major ports on the trade routes to and from London and out to the continent via Harwich. One and a half miles away, in the tiny hamlet of Mistley was the site where the first witch trials took place.

Matthew Hopkins, the son of a preacher, came from a reasonably wealthy family of merchants and was afforded a good education. He went to work in Ipswich as a clerk, with a view to becoming a lawyer. His plans, for some unknown reason, did not succeed so, undaunted, he turned towards the church and the possibility of becoming a preacher. Even this fell on stony ground and nothing more was heard of him until 1645. With two failed careers to his credit, and a need for notoriety possibly fuelled by some complex, twenty-five year old Hopkins turned his attention to the pursuit of witches. He embarked upon a sadistic vendetta which was to make his name dreaded throughout East Anglia and he contributed to part of an international holocaust of such magnitude that it would be another 300 years, during the atrocities of World War II, before anything so inhuman occurred again. In early medieval times the county of Suffolk was referred to as 'The witch country', as it was thought to contain more witches than anywhere else in England.

The Wonders of the Invisible World.

OBSERVATIONS

As well *Historical* as *Theological*, upon the NATURE, th' NUMBER, and the OPERATIONS of the

DEVILS.

Accompany'd with,

I. Some Accounts of the Grievous Molestations, by DÆMONS and WITCHCRAFTS, which have lately annoy'd the Countrey; and the Trials of some eminent *Malefactors* Executed upon occasion thereof: with several Remarkable *Curiosities* therein occurring.

II. Some Counsils, Directing a due Improvement of the terrible things, lately done, by the Unusual & Amazing Range of EVIL SPIRITS, in Our Neighbourhood: & the methods to prevent the *Wrongs* which those *Evil Angels* may intend against all sorts of people among us, especially in Accusations of the Innocent.

III. Some Conjectures upon the great EVENTS, likely to befall, the WORLD in General, and NEW ENGLAND in Particular; as also upon the Advances of the TIME, when we shall see BETTER DAYES.

IV. A short Narrative of a late Outrage committed by a knot of WITCHES in *Swedeland*, very much Resembling, and so far Explaining, *That* under which our parts of *America* have laboured!

V. THE DEVIL DISCOVERED: In a Brief Discourse upon those TEMPTATIONS, which are the more Ordinary *Devices* of the Wicked One.

By **Cotton Mather.**

Boston Printed by *Benj. Harris* for *Sam. Phillips.* 1693.

Title-page of a witch hunt pamphlet by Cotton Mather.

Matthew Hopkins set up headquarters at the Thorn Inn at Mistley, which was an old coaching stop on the London route. It was here, in the upstairs rooms, that he conducted most of his business. His method was to collect gossip and innuendo and meet with people who were prepared to make allegations against their neighbours. These allegations were then turned into formal accusations of Devil-worship and witchcraft.

Right: The Thorn
Hotel, Mistley 1905.

Left: Area of the Witchfinder General's HQ at the Thorn
Hotel, Mistley.

Right: The Thorn
Hotel, Mistley 1997.

THE ILLUSTRATED GUIDE TO WITCHCRAFT

Left: A deep pool where suspected witches were trussed up for the ordeal of 'Swimming'.

Below: Implement of restraint used to punish witches (Iron neck collar).

His first denunciations concerned eleven elderly women in Manningtree and Mistley, all of whom were subsequently hanged. His allegation was that he had become aware of a coven working in the vicinity who knew of his intentions, so they had sent angry spirits to plague him. One of these spirits was in the form of a giant bear, which was instructed to kill him.

Hopkins' name began to be synonymous with the work he was doing. Surrounding towns and town councils who now decreed that they also had problems with witches, invited him into their areas. This extended his working jurisdiction as far as the county of Huntingdonshire.

It does not seem that his sole accomplishment was to succeed in his mission, for now the entire sordid business was encouraged by the financial rewards that he was receiving. For each witch that was brutally

Top: The ordeal of trial by 'Swimming'.

Above: Signature of Matthew Hopkins.

eliminated he was paid a sizeable sum, which no doubt acted as an added incentive.

Early on in the persecutions, Hopkins began to acquire people to help him. Two of his trusted confederates who remained with him for two years were Mary Phillips, an ex-midwife and a gentleman called John Stearne, who was another failed preacher.

Stearne's barbaric method was to stick bodkins and needles into the body of a naked witch to try and find the 'Witches' Mark'. It was believed that when someone became a witch, the Devil placed an invisible type of birth-mark on the body, so if a sharp implement were stuck into that mark, and there was no bleeding, then that person was a witch. John Stearne was so painstaking in his work that he would continually stick bodkins and needles into the victim's body until he found an area that did not bleed. At this point, the victim was declared a witch and hanged.

Several other repugnant techniques of torture were adopted to secure confessions. For example, women were beaten for days on end. Bearing in mind that these were often elderly people, it is not at all surprising that they would confess to anything to put an end to the agony – in fact, death came as a pleasant relief.

'Swimming the witch' was another technique widely used, especially by Hopkins. This would involve tying the thumbs to the big toes, then the naked body was trussed up with a rope around the waist and finally thrown into a river or deep pool. The idea was that if they sank, they were a good Christian, but if they floated, the water had rejected them and they were identified as a witch. The lame excuse given for this was that the water did not want this impure object floating in it. Hanging seems to have been the ultimate penance chosen by Hopkins and his associates for their victims, as only 3-4 burnings are known to have taken place in East Anglia.

One trial that took place even before Matthew Hopkins came on the scene was that of Mother Lakeland from Ipswich, during the mid 1500s. The case was based on the idea that if a woman used witchcraft to murder her husband, then this was classified as treason with a penalty of death by fire.

Matthew Hopkins and his two associates continued to travel the country deriving pleasure from the power, reputation and handsome profit connected with their cruel enterprise. In two short years, over 200 men and women suspected of being witches were put to death. It is known that at Chelmsford Assizes, no fewer than 17 were hanged in a mass execution in one day. Children were often forced to watch their mothers being put to death for witchcraft. Sometimes the children were also killed, because it was believed that witchcraft was hereditary.

Although Hopkins and his cronies were responsible for the death of so many people in their particular area, this was only one region where the hysteria of persecution was prevalent. In Scotland, as in France and

Top: 17th century instruments of torture used at the Bamburg witch trials.

Above: a 17th century engraving showing Matthew Hopkins with witches and their familiars.

Right:
The unmarked grave where Matthew Hopkins is allegedly buried.

Below right:
A blackened skull. This skull was chopped off and thrown into a cauldron of boiling tar. Since this skull was recovered it has had a history of screaming.

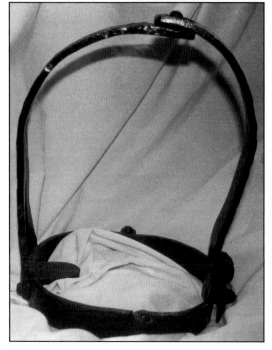

Left: Iron hemet. This was a head restraint for witches. The metal piece protruding inwards held down the tongue.

Germany, the practice of witch burning was adopted, either by burning individuals at a stake, or by throwing the bodies of several witches onto blazing tar barrels.

Sometimes, as an act of mercy, condemned witches were strangled first and occasionally their death would be accompanied by their familiar, a cat or dog, for it was believed that the animal was a spirit and should also be destroyed.

Sometimes, as an act of mercy, condemned witches were strangled first and occasionally their death would be accompanied by their familiar, a cat or dog, for it was believed that the animal was a spirit and should also be destroyed.

The Witchwood by Peter E. Pracownik

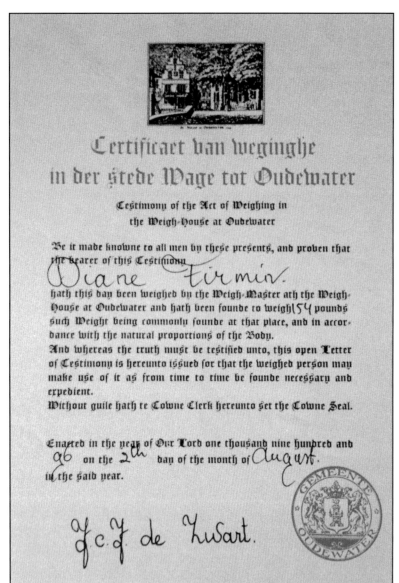

Above:
The actual certificate
which exonerated a
suspect
from an accusation of
witchcraft.

Ireland's history of witch trials is sparse. The only one recorded is of Dame Alice Kyteler, a wealthy aristocrat who had been married many times. On the assumption that the reason that she had gone through so many husbands was because she was doing away with them, the Bishop of Ossory denounced her as a witch. She was arrested with her friends and servants who were also allegedly part of a coven. Some of them were horsewhipped until they confessed to her working with a spirit called 'Robin Artison', who was believed to be a magical being. Dame Alice refuted all knowledge of witchcraft, thumbed her nose at the Bishop and fled, never to be seen again.

The test to determine the authenticity of a witch on the Isle of Wight and the Isle of Man was somewhat different. On these islands, an empty barrel was found, then knives were pushed through the side towards the centre. The witch was placed in the barrel which was then rolled down a steep hill. If she was still alive when she reached the bottom, she was innocent. This was not considered an execution, merely a test.

The last occasion when a person was condemned to death for witchcraft in England took place in Hertford. The unfortunate lady was a Jane Wenham of Walkern, who had, apparently, long held a reputation in her village for being a wise-woman. This seemed to annoy her, and in 1712 she complained to a magistrate that a local farmer was calling her a witch. The parish priest was brought in as a mediator and suggested that the farmer should pay her one shilling as compensation for the insult. Jane was not content with this and began to use her magical powers against the clergyman and his household. His servant fell mysteriously ill and he was pestered by a persistent noise of cats outside his door. The whole village was profoundly disturbed by these happenings. Eventually Jane was brought to trial at Hertford Assizes before Chief Justice Powell, a man of common sense who ridiculed the whole idea of witchcraft.

The jury, however, was of a different opinion and despite the summing-up and direction of the judge, found Jane Wenham guilty. Judge Powell had no choice but to condemn her to death, but through his influence she was later given a royal pardon.

There are accounts from Europe in the mid 1500s of entire villages of men, women and children being executed for witchcraft by the witch-hunters. The chances are that these mass executions were carried out for political reasons, witchcraft being the excuse, as a condemned witches' lands were forfeited to the crown. Many accusations were used, no matter how weak, to secure a conviction and burn a witch.

Above:
Witch weighhouse in Oudewater, Holland.

During the 1500s, in Holland, there were several feeble reasons given as so-called proof of witchcraft and sorcery. A summer hailstorm destroying the harvest would be enough, or if a child died very young, someone was suspected of giving it the evil eye. If cows suddenly gave less milk or if neighbours had a difference of opinion, all of these would be the basis of an accusation of witchcraft. Different methods were used in different parts of Holland during these times of persecution. In the town of Oudewater, trial was either by water, i.e. 'Swimming the witch', or by fire (when the suspect had to walk on hot cinders) or by weighing. The latter arose from the belief that witches were supposed to be light, otherwise they would never be able to fly on their broomsticks.

When a suspect came in to be weighed she was searched for any heavy objects

and stripped. Her height and build was then taken into account. If the weight corresponded to the build of her body, the woman was given a certificate and acquitted of witchcraft for the rest of her life. People came from Poland, Hungary, Germany, indeed from all over Europe, to obtain the highly coveted certificate. Even today, the 500 year-old weighing machine in the witch weigh-house is still used by visitors.

Diane Firmin, a witch of long standing, attended a witchcraft convention in Oudewater in 1996. Hundreds of witches from all over the world were there, many of them undertaking the weighing trial. When the weigh-master gave Diane her certificate of exoneration, she insisted that she was a witch and had been for many years. Her declaration was not accepted and she was told that the scales never lie.

The worst recorded figures for witchcraft persecution came from Scandinavia, where more than half a million were put to death. Executions for witchcraft, or those that used witchcraft as an excuse, were widespread

Above:
Diane Firmin.
A witch for
many years.

Right: In England
witches were
prosecuted by the
civil courts and
hanged
for their crimes; on
the continent they
were usually
prosecuted by
ecclesiastical courts
and burned at the
stake
(A: Hangman; B:
Bellman; C: Two
Sergeants;
D: Witchfinder
taking money for his
work).

throughout Italy, Spain, Switzerland, Holland, Belgium and Germany.

The Vehrmacht became the recognised German equivalent of the Spanish Inquisition, pursuing witches with as much fanaticism as any other country. In Germany and Spain, where it was customary to burn witches, there are accounts of so many people being burned in one day that the dense, pungent smoke would leave buildings covered in human fat.

Russia was a Pagan country until the 12th century. As a result of the later arrival of Christianity there, witchcraft was not seen as a sinister threat, so the hysteria and persecution did not come about before the late 17th century.

One of the last outbreaks of witchcraft panic and definitely the largest in America, occurred between 1692 and 1693 in Salem, Massachusetts. In one year 141 people were arrested in Salem on the pretext of being witches. Of these, 19 were hanged and one pressed to death. Many explanations have been offered for this outbreak of hysteria. One theory is that various rich land-owners used their daughters to accuse others of witchcraft, so that after their death, their land would be sold off cheaply. Whatever the reason, there is little doubt that those involved believed that witchcraft posed a serious threat to the health and well-being of the colony.

A conservative estimate of the number executed for witchcraft has been put at between 3 - 4 million The irony is that only a small percentage of these unfortunate people were genuine witches following the magic of their craft.

No lesson has been learned from this terrible time. Witches survived and continued to practice their rituals. Today, they are not considered to be as much of a threat as they were in the past, but a feeling of persecution is not unfamiliar to modern witches.

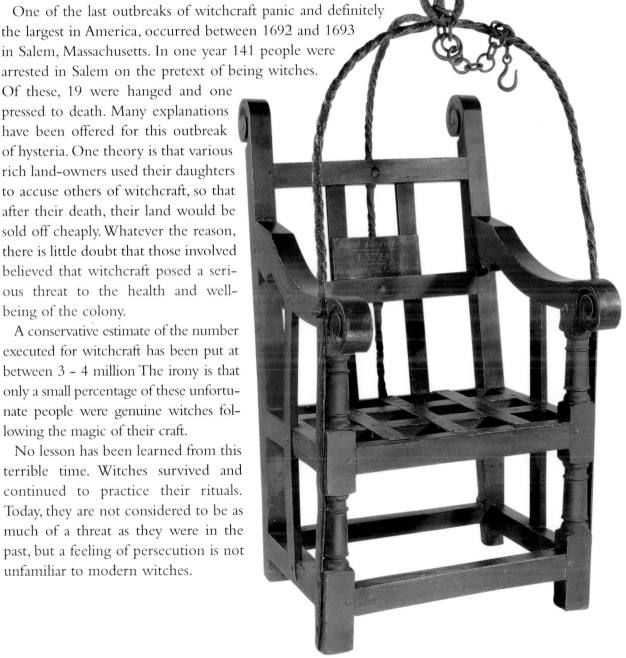

Below:
Ducking chair, 1579.

CHAPTER NINE

THE REVIVAL OF WITCHCRAFT

Above:
Aleister Crowley.

It is not strictly accurate to state that the religion of witchcraft experienced any period of revival. What actually took place was that nearly half a century ago witchcraft started to become more organised.

Even the 'Burning Time' had failed to put down a craft whose roots are in the beginning of time. All that happened was that witchcraft was driven underground, where it became more secretive as a result of the oppression, for there is no doubt that the persecutions had left an indelible mark of fear upon all those who practiced the craft.

Any revival in this century must be associated with those who publicly spoke out, wrote about or performed the intricacies of witchcraft. Because of their actions, whether they were condemned or not, it was obvious that the craft had not been supressed. The wise-woman still existed, covens flourished and ceremonial magic retained its mystery.

Aleister Crowley, denounced in the 1920s as 'The Wickedest Man In The World', did much to publicise black magic and the occult through his noto-

Above:
The witch Sybil Leek with her
jackdaw, Mr Hotfoot Jackson.
Right:

Aleister Crowley's chalice.

riety. Born in Warwickshire in 1875, Aleister Crowley was brought up within a strict Plymouth Brethren family of devout Christians. During his life he seems to have gone out of his way to shock. His behaviour as a child caused his mother to call him the 'Spawn of Satan'. Although it is true that he participated in the darker side of occult practice, most of the bad publicity that surrounds Crowley has been generated by authors who did not really know him. This has led to the belief that he was some sort of Devil incarnate. The attitudes of those who did know him ranged from hatred to admiration for his work, magical capabilities and unorthodox methods.

A witch who knew him very well, at the turn of the century, was Sybil Leek, from the New Forest in Hampshire. Her family entertained many distinguished guests, including H. G. Wells and the controversial Aleister Crowley. Sybil first met him when she was eight years old, and remembered him as a

Aleister Crowley was brought up within a strict Plymouth Brethren family of devout Christians.

Above:
The witch
Sybil Leek

Right:
Witches'
cloak.

good-looking man in his 30s. She vividly described his penetrating eyes and tremendous animal magnetism. When he talked about occultism, magic and astrology he mesmerised his audience and when he had almost exhausted them with the enchantment of his voice, he would suddenly change and lapse into a deep, black mood.

Crowley taught Sybil that words were important in witchcraft, but not only for their meaning. It was the sound that mattered, for each sound sets up a magical vibration. In witchcraft, words are often replaced by strange sounds which appear meaningless to the uninitiated, but undoubtedly help to raise

Clockwise, right to left: The Magician's room at Castletown; The
Witches' cottage at Castletown;
The Old Mill, Castletown; The Wishing Well, Castletown;
Display cabinet, Castletown.

psychic forces and often induce a state of trance.

Sybil became a hereditary witch under the guidance of her psychic Russian grandmother. She was initiated into the craft in George du Loup, Southern France, in the hills above Nice. According to Sybil, she was initiated to replace an elderly Russian aunt who had been high priestess of a coven and who had died.

She wrote extensively about the craft after settling in the New Forest village of Burley, where, by the 1950s she had attained the position of high priestess. After living among the gypsies for some time she joined the 'Horsa' coven, which claimed to have existed for 700 years. She could often be seen walking through the village wearing a long black cloak, with her pet jackdaw, Mr Hotfoot Jackson, perched on her shoulder.

The New Forest area holds a particular significance for witches. The power of their magic was thought to have been exercised during a crucial stage of World War II. On the eve of Lammas (July 31st) , when it was believed that Hitler was about to mount operation 'Sealion', the invasion of Britain, a mass gathering of covens took place. The intention was to magically repel Hitler's invading forces. It is alleged that the dedication of the witches during that mammoth all-night ritual was so great that it resulted in the death, from exhaustion, of several elderly coven members.

Operation 'Sealion' was abandoned because of stormy conditions and a dense fog which mysteriously descended upon the channel and prevented the invasion forces from embarking. No-one can be sure whether or not the New Forest magic was responsible. . . .

Shortly after the war Cecil Williamson, an enthusiastic collector of bizarre curios, opened a Museum of Magic and Witchcraft in a 400 year-old farmhouse in Castletown on the Isle of Man. This exhibition, originally named the The Folklore Centre, was housed in premises known as 'The Witches' Mill' and was intended to be an international centre for modern practicing witches.

The mill acquired its name because the famous Arbory witches lived nearby and the story goes that when the old mill was burnt out, in 1848, they used the ruin as a dancing-ground. It was eminently suited for this purpose.

Above:
Gerald B. Gardner

It was round inside which easily accommodated the witches' circle and the remains of the stone wall screened them from the wind and prying eyes.

A man who was to become known as the father of witchcraft through his key role in its revival, in England and much of the world, in the 1950s was Gerald B. Gardner. His family tree reveals that he was descended from Grissell Gardner who was burned as a witch in 1610 at Newburgh.

Gardner was a much travelled man who, during a period in the Far East,

became acquainted with the natives and studied their spiritual beliefs. He became so fascinated by ritual daggers and knives that he wrote a book on the subject while he was in Singapore. It was while working there for the British government as a rubber plantation inspector and customs official that he developed an interest in archaeology. On his retirement from government work in 1936, he embarked upon various archaeological trips around Europe and Asia Minor.

In Cyprus he visited sites which, he was certain, had appeared in his dreams. This convinced him that he was revisiting areas associated with a previous life. This strengthened his beliefs as he felt that it was substantial proof of reincarnation. Upon returning to England, he and his wife Donna moved into the New Forest area where he became acquainted with people who introduced him to the craft. Just before World War II began, Gardner was initiated into a coven by Old Dorothy Clutterbuck, the coven's high priestess. Little more is known of Gardner's activities during the war.

In 1946 he was introduced to Aleister Crowley who had once been involved in witchcraft - allegedly in one of 'Old George' Pickingill's covens. Gardner admired Crowley and incorporated some of Crowley's material into his own. He intended to write publicly about the survival of witchcraft but at that time it was still illegal in England. Instead he wrote about the craft in a novel, High Magic's Aid, which was published in 1949 under the pseudonym 'Scire'.

The Devil carrying a witch off to hell (Olaus Magnus, Historia de Gentibus Septentrionalibus, 1555).

Right: The cottage used by Gerald Gardner for coven rituals at Bricket wood, Hertfordshire.

In 1951, when the law against witchcraft was repealed, Gardner broke away from the New Forest coven and formed one of his own. That same year he went to Castletown and entered into partnership with Cecil Williamson at the already established Museum of Witchcraft. It was not long before a conflict of personalities set them against each other and when the situation became intolerable, they parted company.

Williamson took his share of artefacts and opened another Museum of Witchcraft at Bourton-on-the Water in Gloucestershire. He remained there for a few years but he was constantly opposed by the local people who, at one time, strung up a dead cat outside his premises as a warning.

He then opened the museum at Windsor, in Berkshire but the duration of his stay had already been determined. He was visited by two grey-suited gentlemen, believed to be from the palace, who informed him that the material displayed in his museum was not considered suitable for a royal town, and he was asked to move on.

In 1960, 50 year-old Williamson chose a site in the village of Boscastle, in Cornwall. He felt that it would be be a more congenial location and, given its tradition of myths and folklore, an acceptable county in which to set up his museum. He remained there for the next 26 years.

'Old George' Pickingill.

During the time that Williamson had been pursuing his quest to establish a permanent museum, Gerald Gardner had also been active with his teaching and writings on the craft. For the first time, books became available which helped the public to learn and understand more about the religion of witchcraft. He devised a beautiful ritual, including the all-important procedure of opening a circle, and made it a part of his teaching. This helped other witches to perfect their own ritual techniques.

In 1953 Gardner initiated Doreen Valiente into his coven and from 1954 – 1957 they collaborated on writing both ritual and non-ritual material. They

The Four Witches (Albrecht Durer, 1497).

Left:
The witch,
Doreen Valiente.

established a body of work which continues to stand as the authority for what became known as the Gardnerian movement.

Gardner's first non-fiction book *Witchcraft Today*, was published in 1954 and became an immediate success. This led to new covens springing up all over England and as a result of the publicity that followed, the press termed him 'Britain's Chief Witch'. After the death of his wife Donna in 1960

Left:
Ceremonial mask.

Gardner's health began to deteriorate and at the age of 76 he had become frail and subject to attacks of asthma. The day-to-day running of his Castletown museum was now left in the capable hands of Campbell and Monique Wilson. Monique, known as Lady Olwen, was Gardner's High Priestess and conducted weekly coven meetings at Gardner's cottage.

Three years later, Gardner met Raymond Buckland, an Englishman who had

Above: Witchcraft Museum, Boscastle.

been initiated into the craft by Monique Wilson and had moved to America. Buckland did much to further the teachings of witchcraft and the Gardnerian tradition in the United States.

While travelling back from Lebanon on 12 February 1964, Gardner suffered a heart attack and died. In his will he bequeathed the museum, ritual tools, artefacts and all his writings to the Wilsons. After a short time they closed the museum and sold much of its contents to the Ripley Museum of Witchcraft and Magic in America, from where it was dispersed to various museums throughout Canada and the United States.

Doreen Valiente, by now a High Priestess, did much in the ensuing years to further the craft with her dedication, books and her knowledge of the Gardnerian tradition. She has always been active in the craft, and renowned for her spiritual enlightenment and compassionate understanding of all aspects of witchcraft past and present, whether it be the workings of solo hereditary witches or covens. Now living in Sussex, she still practices the craft and is often the invited speaker at Pagan Federation assemblies throughout the country.

In 1997 Cecil Williamson, by now 86, decided to sell the witchcraft museum at Boscastle. He felt it was important that it should be taken over by someone who had an understanding of Paganism and was conversant with craft traditions.

Graham King had been running a small industrial business in Hampshire and had been interested in witchcraft and folklore for many years. He decided to take some time off and go on a walking tour of the South of England, visiting as many sacred sites as possible. During this he learned that the museum was on the market. He met with Williamson and after several months of negotiation the deal was finalised and, at the stroke of midnight on Hallowe'en, contracts were exchanged, contrary to a solicitor's normal code of practice.

Graham decided that he wanted to change some of the tableaux in the museum in an endeavour to incorporate an image of the wise-woman of the past, surrounded by the tools of her trade and displayed in an ancient cottage setting. Graham and his partner, Elizabeth Crow, then contacted builders for estimates. They were told that the construction would require three tons of uncut Cornish stone, which was expensive and hard to acquire. One week later, when Graham and Liz had decided that their funds would be inadequate,

Below:
Graham King at the Witchcraft Museum, Boscastle.

a storm blew up, unparalleled in the history of Boscastle. It was of such magnitude that it became necessary to move vehicles and shutter windows against the massive waves that swept up into the harbour and crashed over the museum and surrounding buildings. In the morning, when the sea had receded, Graham went outside to inspect any damage which might have been sustained and there, on his doorstep, was three tons of uncut Cornish stone which had been washed up and deposited there by the fury of the storm.

For the following five months, alterations and improvements were carried out with the aim of re-opening the museum to the public at the Spring Equinox (Ostara, March 21st). Two days before the opening they realised that certain tableaux would be enhanced by a back-cloth drape of magically appropriate colours similar to those often depicted in paintings of auras or chakras.

> Many people have contributed to the progress of witchcraft over the years, with their writing, books and teaching. The museums have played their part by displaying ancient tools and ritual implements to the public. In fact, every witch, traditional or hereditary, and every coven practicing the craft throughout the world have, in their own way, contributed towards the revival and survival of witchcraft.

The only difficulty was that being in such a remote part of Cornwall, their only chance of acquiring the right coloured material would mean a journey to the nearest sizeable city, a round trip of a hundred miles, which would take most of a day, and the one thing that they lacked was time. Instead, Liz decided to load the pick-up truck with sacks of rubbish and take these to the nearby local dump. As she was about to leave the dump and drive away, a flash of colour caught her eye. Upon investigation she found two rolls of coloured material, which were perfect for their needs, sitting on top of a skip of rubbish. Whether these events were luck, a charm that had worked, or a gift from the Gods, we will never know.

Many people have contributed to the progress of witchcraft over the years, with their writing, books and teaching. The museums have played their part by displaying ancient tools and ritual implements to the public. In fact, every witch, traditional or hereditary, and every coven practicing the craft throughout the world have, in their own way, contributed towards the revival and survival of witchcraft.

CHAPTER TEN
WITCHCRAFT'S POPULARITY AS WE APPROACH THE MILLENIUM

Witchcraft is a universal religion of international proportions with its roots in Pagan Europe and its branches spreading throughout the world. Classified as both the oldest and one of the youngest religions, its popularity continues to follow an upward trend.

The Craft, based on ancient practice, has not only stood the test of time but, whenever possible, is still celebrated at sacred sites where witches feel an attachment with the past. This contact with nature and affinity with our ancestors seems to have a growing attraction for today's society, for many people who are not witches can be found seeking a spiritual awakening from the peace and tranquility that can be experienced at these ancient sites. This association with the past does not mean that the craft has

Contact with nature and affinity with our ancestors seems to have a growing attraction for today's society, for many people who are not witches can be found seeking a spiritual awakening from the peace and tranquility that can be experienced at these ancient sites.

Above: Feathered ritual mask.

Above: The old hag of witchcraft with
the magical circle and candles.

remained static throughout the years, even though old rituals, spells and magic
constitute the back-bone of modern witchcraft.

Each 'Book Of Shadows' may well be a comprehensive setting-out of old
procedures and remedies, initiation ceremonies, spells, rituals, charms and
incantations. However, they have been constantly updated throughout the

People are now lookng at their beliefs in a different light. They feel that traditional religions are too concerned with guilt and punishment, whereas witchcraft is a religion of joy and celebration.

The Sabbat, by Goya .

generations as different practices and alternative methods of performing ceremonies are found to be successful.

The wise-woman working alone in her cottage still has an important role to play in today's society. A good example of this is described in a previous chapter, i.e. the witch Cassandra Latham, who is employed by her local hospitals.

Above:
'New Age' shops in
Hertfordshire.

Although a first of its kind, this may well set a trend for the future as alternative medicines and spirtual healing are becoming more accepted practices. This is also addressing the problems posed by a lack of funding for medical services and an increased waiting list of patients.

It is said that nothing is new, it is merely something old that has been recycled. This is especially true in the case of alternative medicine, for many of the potions being administered today are based on remedies used thousands of years ago. These have been formulated and passed on from Indo-European tribes, ancient Chinese doctrines through to North American Indians and, of course, the all-important hedge witches.

Man may have advanced in leaps and bounds technologically, but primitive societies had already discovered answers to problems that we have not yet solved. We can learn a lot by looking back instead of always setting our sights ahead in a kind of forward tunnel-vision. We only have to look at the craze for 'New Age' shops, spiritual and ritual books, crystals, and television and radio programmes about the occult to realise the degree of the public interest in these matters.

People are now lookng at their beliefs in a different light. They feel that traditional religions are too concerned with guilt and punishment, whereas witchcraft is a religion of joy and celebration.

Left:
The burning of the
witches of Mora in
1670. One of the last
manifestations of
witchcraft persecution in
Europe.

Wiccans believe that when a mistake is made it is more constructive to try and
put it right, then learn from it and move on, than to punish oneself.

Witches' concern about the fate of our planet and the depletion of wildlife, is
shared by many. Organisations such as Greenpeace carry out a great deal of
conscientious work in this area.

Recently, tremendous interest has been shown in the survival, cultural history,
and rights of the world's tribal societies, none more so than the Native American
Indians, whose beliefs and rituals have distinct similarities to Wiccan practices.
They lived close to the land and had a respect for the earth and all life upon it.
They totally relied on nature and were at the mercy of the elements in a way
that someone living in modern industrial society would find hard to
understand. So many of these beliefs, that do not change with time, are
encompassed by the Craft and witches feel that adhering to these principles has

become more important as we become aware of the environmental dangers to our planet.

The religion of Wicca has been portrayed as having a fearful past and is still struggling against a belief that it is associated with evil. Despite this, it is becoming more popular. Perhaps this is a sign that the barriers of prejudice are slowly tumbling and that people are starting to make up their own minds about witchcraft.

Increased environmental concern is only one explanation for the upsurge of interest in the Craft. Many people feel that they need to follow a way of relating to the divine without having an intermediary, such as the priest who forgives your sins after confession or the vicar who delivers sermons about fire and brimstone, though this is not to say that witches are anti-Christian. All witches respect the story of Jesus Christ and the gospel of love. In fact, witches respect all Gods and denominations in the belief that you should be free to worship any deity of your choice. Unfortunately, the reverse is not true. The Christian accusation that the witches' Horned God was the Devil, with whom they had made a pact, has been used as anti-Craft propaganda for many years.

Regrettably, this belief has been so well established that adverse criticism and persecution are more prevalent in England than in any other country.

Devotion to the coven and respect for ancient sites have always been a high priority in the Craft. When the field containing the legendary Rollright

Stones on the Oxfordshire/Warwickshire border was recently purchased, the new owners agreed to a continuation of ceremonial rituals there. So covens from Milton Keynes, in Bedfordshire, attended a midnight ritual. During the 90-minute ceremony, lit by candles and the flames beneath the cauldron, High Priest Merlin and his wife, High Priestess Morgana blessed the stones within the cast circle, paying homage to the four quarters and thanking and honouring their ancestors for endowing the site with their magic. The allegiance shown to the Craft on occasions like these has done much to strengthen and augment the popularity of witchcraft in this country today.

Two dedicated English ambassadors of witchcraft were responsible for its introduction into the United States in the early 1960s. Sybil Leek, the English witch and astrologer, moved to New York, then to Los Angeles, finally dividing her time between Houston and Florida. She gained considerable fame by publicising the revival of witchcraft in the western world. As well as her teachings, Sybil wrote over sixty books on the Craft.

Raymond Buckland emigrated to America in 1962 and founded a new tradition of witchcraft, Seax-Wicca. Raymond, and his wife Rosemary, cautiously built up their own coven. Eventually, people around them became impatient, not wanting to wait through the traditional initiation process, so they started their own covens. For over 20 years, Raymond became a leading figure in the witchcraft movement in the United States. Inspired by Gardner's

Above: The inquisition, and other courts, used a variety of torments to elicit confessions of witchcraft. Among the tortures shown here are the strappado, the rack and the water torture.

Witchcraft has always been an inter-national religion and its continuation is assured as we approach the millenium. This assumption is confirmed by the increasing enthusiasm of participating witches and covens in the United Kingdom, Western Europe and America.

Right:
High Priestess Madam Morgana with the Horned God and Goddess at the 'Rollrights'.

Museum of Witchcraft on the Isle of Man, he began collecting pieces for his own museum, which was to be the first one devoted to Witchcraft and magic in America.

Witchcraft caught on quickly in the United States to the extent that (with a certain amount of trepidation) covens began springing up from New York to New Jersey and from Atlanta and Texas to Missouri. In North Carolina in the 1970s, Gavin and Yvonne Frost, two initiated witches originally from England, were the first to establish a church of Wicca in America. They also brought out a bi-monthly publication of the church and school of Wicca entitled *Survival*. The Frosts held well-attended seminars through-out the country, and their school for witches has never lacked enthusiastic recruits.

Witchcraft has always been an international religion and its contin-uation is assured as we approach the millennium. This assumption is con-firmed by the increasing enthusiasm of partici-pating witches and covens in the United Kingdom, Western Europe and America. However, hundreds of years of prejudice and persecution cannot be stamped out overnight.

As a prominent American witch once said, "You know the message is getting through. In another Twenty years, who knows? But we can't afford to give up now. The battle is not nearly won. It still needs an ongoing effort to break the stubborn hold of domineering hierarchical systems and replace them with horizontal linking systems."

The *Survival* publication in North Carolina featured a poem in their May/June edition in 1992, which reflects the feeling of witches all over the world.

Right: 'New Age' shop at Glastonbury.

Long ago and far away
We worked by night and hid by day
We could not in the open go
Because the church did fear us so
They feared us for our power was true
Because our magick they could not do
And so they cried with evil smirk
Let's burn them all – 'tis Devil's work
And burned they did, and torture too
But still we managed to come through
And so today our path is free
To worship Lord and Lady
We work our rites just as of old
Now in the open, free and bold
We did not change or go away
We tell the world: We're here to stay!